TIDE *Ever* RISING

a novel

MANDI TUCKER SLACK

BONNEVILLE BOOKS
AN IMPRINT OF CEDAR FORT, INC.
SPRINGVILLE, UTAH

ISBN 13: 978-1-4621-1107-7

Published by Bonneville Books, an imprint of Cedar Fort, Inc.
2373 W. 700 S., Springville, UT, 84663
Distributed by Cedar Fort, Inc., www.cedarfort.com

LIBRARY OF CONGRESS CATALOGING-IN-PUBLICATION DATA ON FILE.

Cover design by Angela D. Olsen
Cover design © 2013 by Lyle Mortimer
Edited and typeset by Michelle Stoll

Printed in the United States of America

10 9 8 7 6 5 4 3 2 1

TIDE *Ever* RISING

a novel

MANDI TUCKER SLACK

For my children, Austin, Jaden, Dakota, and little bug—thank you for all the giggles, the hugs, the laughter, and the snuggles. You are the ultimate joy in my life, and I am proud to be your mother. I love you all so very much.

For my husband, Chuck—you've always been the "man of my dreams." Thank you for putting up with all my quirks and silliness. You and I have had so many fun adventures, and I can't wait for more. I love you.

ACKNOWLEDGMENTS

Without the love and support of my family, this book would have never seen the light of day. I am so very grateful for my dear sister and best friend, Candace, for all of her support, for the laughter she brings into my life, and for always being there when I need a listening ear. You always know how to make me smile and touch my heart. I cherish the time we spend together. Love you, Slicker!

A special thanks to my wonderful parents. For my mom, Brenda (1957–2011)—even beyond the veil you continue to inspire my life and touch my heart. You taught me so very much. Thank you for the wonderful memories. Thank you for the countless trips to the desert, the mountains, and ghost towns. You are the inspiration for this book. Without your love and support, I wouldn't be who I am today. You've left such an amazing legacy for me and my children. I love you. For my dad, Scott—thank you for always being there, for all of your support and encouragement, and for never letting me give up. I don't know what I would do without you. I love my daddy.

I would like to thank my amazing grandparents, aunts, uncles, and cousins. Thank you all for your support and love. You bring such joy into my life. The moments we've spent together as a family are priceless. I cherish those memories, and I love you all so very much. For my fantastic mother and father-in-law, and to all my sisters and brothers-in-law—thank you for letting me be a part of such a fun family. Thank you, all of you, for your encouragement through the years as I've struggled to write and share my stories.

Mary and Lyle Britt, Amber Robertson, and Vickie Tucker (Aunt Vickie, I think you've read every story I've ever written, no matter how awful they were. Thank you for your love and encouragement.)—thank you for being my first "editors." Your help was invaluable, and I can't thank you enough for your feedback and efforts to help make this story great. To Kim Zuccato—thanks for all the giggles! I'm so glad you are a part of my life.

I would also like to thank the staff at Cedar Fort and my editor, Michelle Stoll, for giving me a chance to realize my dreams. Without your tireless efforts on my behalf, my books would not be a reality. And to my readers, thank you for taking the time to share in my world of make believe. You have contributed to my growth as an author. I have so appreciated your words of acknowledgement and your efforts to share my books with others. Your support means the world to me.

CHAPTER *One*

*T*hunder grumbled in the distance. The sound seemed to resonate across the rugged hills that surrounded her. The air was cooler, clean and fresh, and Kadence Reynolds enjoyed the crisp breeze after months of excruciating summer heat. She could smell the dust in the air and feel the almost tangible vibrations of electricity humming in the sky above her. A gust of wind whipped her auburn hair into her face. She sighed, and a smile touched her lips when she heard her sister's familiar voice drawing near.

"It's going to rain, Kadie. Can we go now? *Please?*" Maysha Reynolds whined.

Kadie looked up toward the ever-darkening sky. Storm clouds rolled and collided with one another, creating an awe-inspiring picture. She watched the sky for a moment longer before she turned to grin at her younger sister.

"Oh, come on—it's not that bad. We won't melt."

Her sister's eyes widened. "This took me all morning." She pointed dramatically toward her short, sleek-styled hair. "Do you realize how long it takes to smooth out all my curls?"

Kadie rolled her eyes. "Only *you* fix your hair to go out exploring."

"Only *you* enjoy exploring dying old towns and piles of rubble."

"You didn't have to come," Kadie reminded her.

Maysha snorted. "Like I'd send you out here by yourself. You'd fall into some old cellar and break your neck! No one would ever find you."

"You have such an imagination," Kadie laughed, shaking her head.

1

As a junior-high history teacher, Kadie had a hard time hiding her enthusiasm as she gazed across the remnants of the long-abandoned town. She had spent the majority of her summer vacation exploring the various ghost towns across the state, and she wanted to learn firsthand all she could about the unique history of each town. It was a project she had assumed in order to help her future history students imagine life in Utah before television and video games, and Mammoth was her last stop before the school year started. Maysha had finally agreed to come, and Kadie enjoyed the time they were spending together, despite her sister's constant grumbling.

"Oh!" Maysha gingerly made her way up the crumbling stairs of the old foundation.

Only two walls stood, framing the hills beyond the skeleton of a once-grand home. An old chimney sat in the middle of the floor, and the crumbling brick lay broken and decaying on the stained, debris-covered cement. Thunder sounded loud above the hills. Kadie laughed, disappearing behind a wall to explore the next section of the ruined home. Maysha suddenly yelped, and Kadie turned to watch as her sister stepped around the wall, brushing furiously at a few clinging strands of cobweb. Sighing, Kadie glanced around. A flash of white caught her eye, and triumphantly she bent to retrieve a small shell button peeking out from the rubbish.

Taking a moment to study the old button, she smiled before placing it carefully in her pocket. She jumped from the foundation and gazed further down the old dirt road. Another ruin sat in the distance, and she could tell that a few walls still remained. Her eyes narrowed as she studied the crumbling structure just as a breeze brushed past, causing a cloud of dust and dead leaves to swirl about the abandoned home.

Feeling intrigued, she turned to Maysha. "One more," she begged, pointing down the road. "Just *one* more? That's all, and then we'll go. I want to see that place."

Maysha's shoulders sagged, and she looked at Kadie crossly. "Promise?"

Kadie nodded. "Last one."

"Oh, alright, fine! But I mean it—last one. I can't believe I agreed to come out here."

Kadie chuckled and helped Maysha down from the foundation before she turned and hurried toward the narrow dirt lane leading to the next ruin. She stepped around several clumps of knee-high sagebrush and then turned once again to watch as Maysha cautiously made her way across the rough terrain.

"Ow—oh—*ouch*!" Maysha complained.

She stumbled, and Kadence grinned. "Why on earth did you wear sandals? I told you to bring boots."

"I don't believe I own *hiking* boots. When I agreed to come, you said we were going to look at old *houses*, not go wandering around in piles of rubble and brick. What can you *possibly* find so interesting out here? What are we looking for?"

Thoughtfully, Kadie stepped up into the crumbling structure of what must have once been a small, modest home. She was surprised to discover areas where much of the wooden flooring was still intact. Standing on the edge of the cement foundation, she gazed around the home.

"I don't really know," she confessed. "I just find it . . . fascinating. It's interesting, I guess. You know, seeing how people must have lived thirty, forty, fifty years ago. Each town has its own unique feel—its own personality." She turned to face Maysha. Her sister's eyes were incredulous and Kadie smiled sheepishly. "I found a button."

"Oh—*goodie*!" Maysha responded. "You know it's wrong to get a thrill off of finding dead people's garbage."

Kadie chuckled, shaking her head. She turned back to face the ruined home. Examining the standing walls, she noticed charred wood, and burned beams lay strewn across the rotting wood floor. No part of the roof remained intact.

"This place had a fire at one point," Kadie mused. "Maybe you'd better not come up," she called to Maysha.

Kadie eyed the floor warily. A conglomeration of rusty nails protruded from the rotting wood. She picked her way around a large pile of burned timber. The old, wood flooring squeaked and groaned under her weight as she worked her way through the ruined home. She glanced around wonderingly.

"This must have been the kitchen," Kadie reflected.

A stained, cracked porcelain basin still stood against a partial wall. Bits and pieces of the rotted linoleum countertop were still in place. Broken glass, dead leaves, and empty beer cans littered the floor. With the toe of her boot, she removed a thick layer of debris to expose the original, checkered linoleum floor. She turned to check on Maysha, who still hovered near the crumbling stairs.

"This is a newer house, I think," she called, "maybe thirties or forties."

Kadie ran her hand across the smooth porcelain of the sink. Careful to avoid more broken beer bottles and shattered windows, she worked her way to the opposite side of the house. The smell of charred wood still lingered. Had the fire destroyed the home? Or had vandals burned the house after it had been abandoned? She shivered when a sudden gust of wind tore through the ruin. Several rain drops fell onto her head and shoulders. She wrapped her arms across her chest and gazed up toward the swollen clouds.

Another burst of wind rushed past, causing the old timbers and bricks to groan. She eyed the charred, decaying walls. This place felt different than the last; more eerie and . . . she couldn't quite think of the word—more alive? She inhaled sharply then turned when she heard the sound of her name carried on the wind. Gooseflesh caused her hair to stand on end, and her breath caught in her throat. She could hear the wind sighing through the pinion pines close by. A window pane, hanging from a loose nail, squeaked as the breeze caressed her cheek.

"Maysha?" she called, feeling uncertain. "Did you call me?"

"What? No!" her sister returned. "Look, can we go now? We're going to be soaked before we get back to the car. And besides, I think I left my window down."

Kadie exhaled and shivered visibly. She couldn't quite shake the feeling that she was being watched. *This house definitely feels different than the last*, she thought. Feeling uneasy, she turned back toward Maysha. She entered the kitchen area again, glancing cautiously behind her.

"Alright, I'm coming. You know, I—whoa!" Kadie's foot fell through a loose patch of linoleum flooring. She stumbled and fell to the floor, nicking the palm of her hand on several small shards of broken glass. "Oh . . . ," she murmured, eyeing her cut hand. She brushed the dirt and glass from off her palm and then turned to carefully pull her foot out of the splintered wooden floor. "Great." She frowned and eyed the small circle of blood spreading around a tear in the fabric of her jeans.

"What did you do? Are you all right?" Maysha stepped toward the crumbling, stone steps.

"I'm fine!" Kadie called.

She didn't want Maysha to risk cutting herself or stepping on a rusty nail. *Besides,* Kadie mused, *there's no sense in both of us needing a tetanus shot.*

Kadie pulled the cuff of her jeans up to better examine her leg. A jagged scratch oozed blood that dripped onto her sock. She pulled the leg of her jeans back into place then stood. A flash of light caught the corner of her eye and she paused. Startled, she turned to face the jagged hole her foot had created and was surprised when she noticed an object just beyond the cobwebs. Curiously she knelt and peered into the opening. Careful to avoid the glass and rusty nails, she pulled at the rotting wood and linoleum, clearing the space.

"Ugh!" she yelped when her fingers came in contact with a thick web, and she watched with wide eyes as a black widow spider scurried away. She cringed then sighed.

"What is it? Aren't you coming?" Maysha called.

"Just a second," Kadie responded. "I think I found something."

Using a stick, she cleared the cobwebs and carefully reached into the hole to remove a rusty coffee can. Dust and dead leaves clung to the old can, and she brushed them away excitedly.

"What is it?" Maysha shouted again, sounding more impatient.

The can, though rusty in spots, still showed the original yellow paint and black lettering clearly. She clasped the can in her hands and shook it gently. The contents clanged and thumped within, and she grinned. Whatever was inside were definitely not coffee grounds. The sound of Maysha's footsteps caught her attention, and she turned to face her sister.

"Be careful. Seriously, there are a lot of nails and broken glass," she cautioned.

"What did you find?" Maysha asked, coming to kneel beside Kadie. "Don't tell me it's another button!" Just then, she caught sight of Kadie's bloody jeans. She scowled. "I knew you were going to get hurt wandering around places like this."

Kadie shrugged. "It's only a scratch. Anyway," she laughed, flourishing the can, "look, it's old, much older than the house even. I've seen some like this before in antique stores. They're worth a lot, and it's in great shape considering its age."

Maysha pulled a face, taking the can from Kadie. "A coffee can—great. Is there anything in it?" she asked, shaking the can. Her eyes narrowed and she frowned. "And . . . it's a bunch of rocks."

Kadie chuckled when Maysha pulled on the metal lid, and her sister scowled when it wouldn't give. Kadie reached for the can. Taking it from her sister, she twisted the old metal lid. Her brow knit when the cover stuck and she glanced around the room. Grasping a broken brick, she used it to tap the sides of the cover. Rust-colored dust fell onto her hand. She brushed it off onto her jeans before she tried to twist the lid again. It turned, the metal grating as the years of rust gave way. The cover came off, and they peered inside with eager expressions.

"A book?" Maysha asked, sounding disappointed.

Kadie reached in excitedly. She pulled out a withered leather-bound book. It was small, and the pages were warped and yellowed with age. Carefully, she opened the book to the first page. The ink had faded some, but she could easily make out the hand-written words.

"April 4, 1935," Kadie began, her eyes widening with anticipation. "Baked a peach pie today. Mama said it tasted real good. Papa came home late today. He'd been out to Delta. Said Uncle Frank had to close his shop. He extended so much credit he just couldn't stay in business no more.

"Adelaide and I traded eggs in town today for some socks for Alvin. He wore his clean out. Little Ruthie took ill this afternoon. We had no money to pay Doc Reilly. I don't believe he would have taken pay had Mama and Papa had it to give. He checked Papa's leg too. I promised to bake him a peach pie."

"April 7, 1935," Kadie went on. "Little Ruthie's fever broke this afternoon. Papa and Bishop gave her a blessing late last night. We were all real scared for her. Doc Reilly stopped by this afternoon and said she was on the mend." Kadie stopped. She glanced at Maysha wonderingly. "It's a journal. This is so . . . ," she paused, then exclaimed, "Amazing! I can't believe this book survived for so long." She flipped carefully through the yellowed pages. "Look, the entries go into December."

"Wow," Maysha breathed.

She turned and grabbed the can, dumping the rest of the contents onto the floor. A silver quarter rolled onto the linoleum, followed by a wad of yellowed fabric. Maysha unrolled the fabric to reveal a tarnished silver pendant. A red jewel, fastened in the middle of a large, intricate oval-shaped design, shone brilliantly, despite its age.

Maysha's mouth fell open. "Cool!" she exclaimed.

"It's beautiful," Kadie murmured, taking the charm in her hands to study its unique design.

"Okay, I'll admit, this is really neat." Maysha touched the pendant. "Do you think it's real?"

Kadie laughed. "No, I don't think so. It's only costume jewelry. It's very pretty though."

The loud, resonating sound of thunder suddenly caused both Maysha and Kadie to jump. Kadie laughed a bit breathlessly and looked up at the angry sky. The black clouds churned directly above them. "I think we should go now."

Maysha eyed the bloated clouds overhead and stood while Kadie gathered the contents of the can. She reached for the quarter and the journal and wrapped the pendant back inside the worn fabric before she placed all the trinkets back inside. She screwed the rusty lid in place and tucked the can under her shirt, then brushed the dirt and crushed dead leaves from off her jeans.

"Do you think if we stay, we'd find more?" Maysha asked. She glanced around with excited eyes.

Kadie frowned. "Now you want to stay?" She smirked and pointed toward the sky.

Maysha eyed the somber clouds and grimaced. "Well then, lets come back next weekend," she suggested as they worked their way out of the old ruin and back toward the dirt road.

Kadie laughed aloud as another boom crashed overhead, releasing a torrent of rain. Despite rushing, they were both thoroughly wet when they reached the car. Maysha's brow furrowed when they slid into the vehicle, and she eyed her reflection despairingly.

"My hair," she lamented.

Kadie chuckled, placing the can in the backseat while Maysha started the little Mazda sedan. They drove Highway Six back toward the main section of town, and Kadie was, once again, amazed when they entered the small, nearly unpopulated city-center of Eureka.

"This is such a neat place," she murmured, then "Oh!" she exclaimed when she caught sight of a crude, historic cabin set further back from the road. "Pull over. I have to see this!"

Maysha pulled the Mazda to the side of the road, and Kadie exited the vehicle. Maysha followed, and they waited patiently for a single car to pass.

"Busy place," Maysha remarked dryly.

They crossed the street and stepped over to the cabin. "Wow!" Kadie exclaimed. She pulled her camera from her purse. She took a few shots while Maysha looked on with a bored expression.

"Oh, wow! This cabin might have actually belonged to Porter Rockwell," Kadie called.

"Who?" Maysha asked, uninterestedly.

"Porter Rockwell. You seriously don't remember who Porter Rockwell is?" Kadie's mouth hung open.

Maysha's eyebrows rose. "No."

"He was Joseph Smith's and Brigham Young's personal bodyguard. I can't believe you don't remember."

"Oh, yeah, isn't he that guy that couldn't cut his hair or something like that? You know, like Samson?"

Kadie grinned. "These pictures will be great. The kids will love these." She took a few more photos of the inside of the cabin while Maysha wandered down the sidewalk. "I'm done," Kadie called after a few moments.

Maysha turned and pointed down the sidewalk toward a gas station. "Great. Let's head down here. I'm starving. I want a drink and some snacks before we head back."

As they entered the small service station, an older woman greeted them with a smile. The store accommodated a modest selection of groceries. Sagging shelves held an assortment of canned goods, toiletries, and snacks. An ancient cooler kept sodas and juices cool. The left side of the store housed a small gift store with a good assortment of antiques scattered in among the new merchandise. Maysha turned toward the snack aisle, while Kadie was immediately drawn into the little gift shop. "Can I help you find anything in particular?" the older store clerk asked kindly.

"No, thank you. I'm just looking. We're touring the town today. This place is amazing. There's so much living history."

The woman smiled. "Oh, there certainly is. There are a lot of places to see and explore. Where are you two visiting from today?"

"Salt Lake," Kadie responded.

Maysha held up a bag of chips. "How much for these?" she called across the store.

"Two-ninety-nine," the clerk answered.

"Great. You want a soda or something, Kadie?"

"Yes," Kadie replied before she turned her attention back to the woman. "Have you lived here long?"

"Oh, yes, several years. Eureka was once the major city of the Tintic back in the day, but that was years ago. By the time my husband and I moved here, it was starting to dwindle, and well—it's remained about like this. There are only a few mines still being worked, but it's a nice little historic town. We enjoy living here."

Kadie smiled and was about to reply when the store's phone rang. The clerk excused herself, stepping back to the counter to answer it. Kadie shrugged and continued studying the array of antiques and bric-a-brac. The full shelves sagged, and she was delighted to discover several old, black-and-white photos hidden in the back row. Curiously, she pulled the largest off the shelf. Studying the photo of an old town, she flipped it over to read the faded writing on the back.

"Dividend—1927," she read.

"What's that?" Maysha came up behind Kadie and peered over her shoulder. "It's a photo of Dividend. It was a smaller mining town, just outside of Eureka."

She placed the photo back in its original spot before she reached for a smaller photo. Several teenaged kids started toward a hidden camera man, their smiles frozen in time and their arms draped across one another's shoulders in a casual manner. They were dressed in their Sunday best. A brick church house stood behind them, and a thick layer of snow blanketed the ground. Kadie studied the photo carefully, as two girls in particular stood out. One girl's hair was cut short, bobbed and curled in the style of the day. The other had long, thick, black hair that flowed freely across her shoulders. The girls' dresses matched, and Kadie realized the two young women were sisters. Maysha leaned in closer and studied the photo before she pointed to the girl on the left with the short black hair.

"Hey, isn't that . . . ," Maysha paused and Kadie's eyes widened when she recognized the pendant hanging around the girl's neck.

"It is—it has to be," Kadie spoke louder than she intended.

"It looks just like our coffee pendant," Maysha mused. "Wow! Now that's just creepy." She backed away from the photo playfully and Kadie laughed, but a sudden shiver coursed up her spine, raising gooseflesh on her arms. The same peculiar feeling she'd experienced earlier while exploring the old house assailed her, and she flipped the photo to read the writing on the back.

" 'Road show—December, 1935. *A Christmas Carol*. Front row: Jack Phillips, Thomas James, and Mildred Cole. Second row: Frances McMullen, Ruby Sams, Charlotte Clarke, and Adelaide Clarke.' They're sisters. They look like twins. They have to be, and this—" she pointed to the girl, "this is Adelaide with the necklace."

"Hmm," Maysha murmured tersely. "Can we go now?"

She turned away and stepped to the register, and Kadie rushed to Maysha's side. She placed the old photo on the countertop and asked the store clerk, "Do you know anything about this picture?"

The woman's eyes narrowed and she studied the photo for a moment. "Let me see . . . oh, yes—this is the young women's and young men's group after a road show production. Road shows were quite popular back then." She pushed the photo back toward Kadie.

"Do you know anything about these two girls here?" she pressed.

The clerk shook her head. "I'm afraid not. It was long before my time."

"Oh, yes, of course. Is it for sale?"

"It's seven dollars if you're interested," the clerk responded.

Maysha's eyes met hers and Kadie smiled knowingly. "I'll take it," she announced. She waited in silence as the clerk placed the photo in a paper sack.

"Thank you." Kadie waved when they turned to leave.

"I can't believe you bought that," Maysha exclaimed once they were outside.

They walked slowly down the sidewalk, and Kadie watched the sky. The sun was trying to peek through the thinning clouds. Maysha handed Kadie her soda when they reached the Mazda. She took a sip and eagerly turned to retrieve the old coffee can from the back seat. The lid came off easily. She dumped the contents onto her lap and removed the necklace. She slid the photo from the bag and held the pendant next to the old black-and-white. They were identical. Kadie reached for the journal, opening to the first few pages.

She scanned the first page before she whispered, "I can't believe this! Listen—'Adelaide and I traded eggs in town today for some socks for Alvin' . . . Adelaide. This journal must have belonged to Charlotte Clarke. That house . . . they must have lived there."

"Put it up, Kadie."

Confused, Kadie glanced toward Maysha. Maysha's shapely brows drew together as she eyed the journal and repeated, "Put it back."

"What? But this is amazing. It—"

"Honestly! Get it out of my sight. This is *creepy*," she argued. "I'm not joking!"

A slow smile touched Kadie's lips, and she shrugged but replaced the contents of the can and carefully placed the photo back inside the paper sack. "I'll admit," her eyes narrowed thoughtfully, "it is kind of weird."

"Yeah—kind of," Maysha muttered as she pulled the Mazda onto Main Street. The little car accelerated, and they sped down Highway Six toward the freeway.

CHAPTER *Two*

I 've probably missed Aaron coming by. I thought we'd be home sooner than this," Maysha complained while she parked the Mazda in the compact parking garage of the apartment complex where they lived.

"I'm sure if he came by . . . well, he'll call soon," Kadie replied. She gathered the can and the photo in her arms before stepping from the car.

"Look at me!" Maysha pulled a face. "I'm a mess! He can't see me like this." She eyed herself critically in the rearview mirror. "I need to hurry and change."

She bolted from the car, and Kadie followed her sister up the stairs to the second story apartment they shared.

"Hurry," Maysha whined while Kadie unlocked the door.

They stepped into the small, cramped living space, and Maysha rushed for the bathroom. Kadie placed her purse on the top of a pile of boxes sitting in the living room, and her shoulders slumped. Maysha had already started packing her belongings. She was getting ready to move back to Provo, where she attended Brigham Young University. Kadie was going to miss her terribly. Maysha was really all she had left, since they had lost their mother early in life.

Kadie had been only twelve when their mother had died of breast cancer. Her father had not had an easy time, but despite raising two teenage girls alone, he had made a good life for Kadie and her sister. Then a little less than a year ago, their father had died of a stroke, leaving her and Maysha on their own. The thought caused her heart to twist, and she sighed. She could hear her younger sister moving about the small bathroom, preparing for her date. What would she do without Maysha around?

"Are you going out with Rob tonight?" Maysha suddenly called through the closed door.

Picking up the coffee can and photo, Kadie moved into the modest dining area. She placed the contents in her arms high onto the bookshelf and eyed her find excitedly. She was eager to read the rest of the journal.

"Kadie," Maysha called impatiently, "did you hear me?"

"Umm . . . no," she returned, "not tonight. Robert has a meeting."

"Too bad." Maysha's voice grew louder as the bathroom door swung open. She came into the dining area, patting a curl in place. "I was hoping you two would come with Aaron and me. We're going to that new restaurant that just opened at the Jordon Commons. Do you want to come?"

Kadie smiled and stifled a yawn. "No thanks," she declined. "I'm going to stay in tonight and relax a bit. Besides, I still have a ton of work to finish up before the school year starts."

Maysha's eyebrows rose critically. "Wow—boring. Alright, if you're sure. Anyway, I doubt dear *Robert* would approve of you coming with us."

Maysha grinned when Kadie scowled. The door bell chimed, and she rushed past Kadie. She blew a kiss in her direction. "Bye—love you," she called as she skipped out the door.

"Have fun."

Silence enveloped the apartment, and Kadie stepped into the kitchen. She yanked open the refrigerator door and eyed the meager contents critically. She exhaled and shut the door before she turned toward the bedroom. The coffee can, sitting high on top of the shelf, caught her attention, and she sighed again. *First my lessons*, she reminded herself as she moved into the bedroom and removed her dusty clothes.

The hot water felt wonderful, and she took her time showering. She liked to be clean after spending the day hiking around cobweb-infested ruins. The day had been eventful, and it felt good to be home where she could relax. She was grateful that Robert had a meeting. Since her engagement, Kadie really hadn't had much time for herself, and a double date with Maysha and Robert in the same room was never a good idea. Robert and her sister knocked heads right from the start, and Maysha made it no secret that she very much disliked Robert Greenly. He and Kadie had dated for nearly a year before he'd proposed, and they had been engaged for nearly as long.

She stepped from the shower. Wiping at the film of moisture on the mirror, she studied her reflection. Her long, auburn hair fell in wet strands down her back, and she gazed into her own hazel eyes. Why was she marrying Robert Greenly? She sighed and reached for her fade cream. She smeared a good amount across the freckles that ran along the bridge of her nose and cheeks, then wrapped a towel around her head and dressed in a pair of comfortable sweats.

With an inward groan, she sat at the kitchen table. She eyed the stack of folders and unfinished lesson plans with a frown. Her stomach growled, and she reached for her cell phone. She placed her order for a medium pizza and then went to hang up.

"Oh," she called into the receiver before she shut the phone, "throw in a two-liter of orange soda, please?" She waited for a response. "Thank you," she replied before she snapped her phone shut.

With a loud whimper, Kadie pulled the stack of work toward her and opened the first folder. She began working on her first lesson plan with little enthusiasm. The apartment was quiet, except for the soothing sound of the freeway in the distance. The clock ticked steadily, and Kadie stifled a yawn. Then without warning, a loud, resounding crash filled the little apartment. Kadie let out a startled scream.

Jumping from her chair, she spun around, breathing fast. Her heart beat against her ribs while she watched the old coffee can roll across the dining room floor. It rolled beneath the table and stopped under her chair. She glanced about the room before her eyes shot toward the bookshelf. She was certain she'd pushed the can back away from the edge. She raised a trembling hand to her throat.

"Okay," she murmured. She bent and grasped the can, then studied the shelf again. "I guess I didn't push it back from the edge," she tried to convince herself.

She took a deep, calming breath as she studied the can curiously.

"I have the rest of the month to finish my lessons," she spoke aloud. Her eyes darted around the apartment, and she suppressed a sudden shiver before she inhaled deeply and turned to sit at the table. She opened the can and retrieved the journal. She eyed the cover with a hammering heart and cautiously opened to the third entry:

July 3, 1935

Ester and Charlie Wilkerson spent the day with us. Mr. Tibble died yesterday. Papa said there had been another cave-in at the mine. A lot of men were hurt. They got them all out, but not Mr. Tibble. Mama is real sad. Mr. Tibble was a good man, and he had two little boys. Mama spent the day with Mrs. Tibble, and Adelaide and I baked bread to take to his family. Ester and Charlie were good company while Mama was away. Doc Reilly examined Papa's leg again. Said it was healing good. Papa should be able to return to the mines in a month or so. Mama looked worried. I know she frets about Papa when he's deep underground.

July 4, 1935

Happy Independence Day! I went to the parade in town with Adelaide, Kirk Oscar, and Ruby Sams. Fred Moss came to the luncheon and asked Adelaide to sit with him. I think he's sweet on Adelaide. She won't say, but I think she's quite taken with him too. He walked Adelaide and I home from the dance tonight. He says he's going to work with the CCC camp. He told Adelaide he's enrolled for six months. He leaves next week. Adelaide was real quiet before she got into bed tonight. I think she's real sad he's leaving.

July 6, 1935 Sunday

At church today, Ruby Sams announced she's to begin study at the University of Utah come fall. I'm green with envy. We've organized the road show troupe again. We have our first recital after Sunday school this week. Jack Phillips will be there. Maybe he'll walk me home.

August 9, 1935

Fred Moss left last week with the CCC camp. Poor Adelaide. She's heartbroken. She confided in me last night that Fred will ask Papa for his blessing. When he returns, Adelaide and I will be seventeen. Papa has his mind set on Adelaide and me attending university. He won't be happy. Clyde Johnson asked me to mid-summer dance. Mama said now that Papa has returned to work, perhaps now I'll get that dress I've been admiring in the J. C. Penny's store. Adelaide and I stopped to look in the window yesterday after school. Mrs. Jukes came out wearing the most ridiculous hat. It probably cost Mr. Jukes a small fortune.

Wouldn't it be fun to put on airs? Just for the day? I'd dress up in the most outrageous fashions, and I'd strut about downtown. Perhaps I'd stroll past Jack Phillips' house. I wonder what he'd say, with me looking like a real lady.

Kadie smiled as she laid the old journal on the table. She yawned and jumped when the doorbell rang. Startled, she hurried to answer the door, realizing she'd forgotten all about her pizza.

"Hi," she greeted the teenage delivery boy.

"It's fourteen ninety-five," the boy replied unenthusiastically.

She rushed into the kitchen to grab her wallet and paid the boy before he shoved the pizza and the two-liter of soda into her hands. Her stomach growled when she smelled the warm cheese.

"Enjoy." The boy turned and descended the stairs.

"Thanks," Kadie called before she shut the door and turned into the kitchen with her dinner.

She examined the open journal as she stuffed a slice of pepperoni pizza into her mouth, then poured herself a glass of orange soda before she moved to the bookshelf. She reached for the old photo as she sipped her drink and smiled.

She felt as if she knew Charlotte and Adelaide personally. Even Ruby Sams and Jack Phillips did not feel like strangers. She still could scarcely believe her good fortune in discovering both the journal and the photo. She downed the rest of her soda and glanced at her computer as an idea formed. She wondered if she'd be able to research Charlotte Clarke or Adelaide. If she searched the genealogy database, perhaps she could discover whether or not Charlotte or Adelaide was still living. If not, maybe she'd find other living relatives. She knew a journal like that belonged with Charlotte's family.

Determined, she grabbed another slice of pizza and sat at her computer. She opened her browser, pulled up a genealogy search engine, and eagerly typed *Charlotte Clarke*. She held her breath while she waited for her slow connection to go through, and she felt amazed when her search brought up several results. She meticulously scanned the list, and her eyes widened when she discovered a listing for Charlotte Clarke born in Eureka, Utah. She checked the name again and read through the available information.

"This has to be her!" Kadie exclaimed, her voice marring the silence of the apartment. "Charlotte Clarke—born 1919 in Eureka, Utah, died in—1935?" She paused and read it again. "She *died* that year?" she asked aloud.

She licked her lips and reached for the journal, flipping carefully to the end, to find the last entry.

December 23, 1935

Adelaide left early with the road show troupe. They won't be back until tomorrow afternoon. They were performing at the Provo Tabernacle tonight. How I'd looked forward to going, but Doc Reilly was firm. I was not to go out and expose my lungs to the frigid air, or I'd surely suffer a relapse of the pneumonia. My lungs feel fine, but Mama frets still.

Papa had a bad row with Mr. Jukes tonight. Mama kept us kids out, but I snuck out back and watched from the kitchen window. I've never seen Papa so angry. Mr. Jukes threatened Papa. He told him he'd be sorry if he ever put that new mine proposal before the Union. Mr. Jukes is planning on running for state senate, and Papa said the new mine proposal would ruin Mr. Jukes' chances of election if word got out that he's really a crook. Papa told Mr. Jukes he wouldn't stand to see hardworking men taken advantage of. He called Mr. Jukes a crook and a liar.

If Mr. Jukes had sprouted horns, I would have believed I was looking at Lucifer himself. He was so red. I thought he'd likely throttle Papa. Mama worried too. She stepped in front of Papa. Adam Jukes stood next to Mr. Jukes. He looked just as mad. He's the same age as Alvin. I've never liked him. Not since he bloodied Alvin's nose just for a good time last spring. Mama told the men they needed to calm down. She told Mr. Jukes she'd call the sheriff if he and Adam didn't get out of our house.

Mr. Jukes told Papa he'd be real sorry if he got in his way. He told Papa to watch his back. I didn't like that. I'm scared for Papa, but he says not to worry. He says Mr. Jukes is a bully and a coward. I hope he's right. Dear Adelaide, I miss her. I hope she has a grand time tonight. I'm going to eat my last chocolate before bed tonight.

Kadie felt bewildered. If the death record was correct that meant Charlotte had died soon after writing her last entry. The last date was only a week before the end of the year. What had happened and how had she died? Had the pneumonia come back? Bewildered, Kadie turned the pages of the journal and began reading the entry before Charlotte's last.

December 12, 1935 Thursday
    Last week I did some mending for Mrs. Acworth, and Mr. Palmer let me do some milking. I finally earned enough to buy Adelaide that charm necklace she's admired in the J.C. Penny's store. When I bought it, I meant it for Christmas morning, but I couldn't wait. I gave it to her yesterday. Today before school, I woke to find all my chores had been done, and a box of chocolates sitting on my pillow. Adelaide had ordered them special from Mr. Underhill's fancy catalogue. When Mama discovered we had given our gifts early, she shook her head.

Setting the journal aside, Kadie dumped the rest of the contents of the can. She placed the quarter next to the journal before she unwrapped the necklace. She studied its unique design. The necklace was obviously just a piece of costume jewelry, but it was beautiful. This had been Charlotte's gift to Adelaide.

She pulled the photo closer and studied Charlotte and Adelaide's smiling faces. What had happened to Charlotte? Kadie could find no record of a death certificate, no cause of death, and no actual date; just 1935. Was Adelaide still living? She faced her computer and typed in *Adelaide Clarke*. She hit enter and waited for the search to finish. She tapped her fingernails against her teeth, then jumped when her phone rang, shattering the silence of the apartment. She rolled her eyes and reached to answer it.

"Hello?" she answered rather impatiently.

"Hi, darling," Robert's familiar voice answered.

"Oh . . . Robert, hi . . ." she responded absently when the list for Adelaide Clarke appeared.

"Kadie?" Robert asked again.

"Oh . . . sorry. I'm kind of busy right now," she replied, feeling frustrated. She was eager to return to her search for Adelaide.

"Are you alright? You don't sound like yourself."

Kadie laughed shortly. "I'm fine. Honestly, I'm just in the middle of something, that's all. How was your meeting?"

"Boring. Mother called. She was wondering if we could come by tomorrow to discuss the menu for the luncheon."

Kadie inhaled and pinched the bridge of her nose. "We already decided on the chicken, didn't we?"

Robert's mother, although well-intended, drove Kadie insane with wedding plans despite the fact that the wedding was another four months away. She rubbed her temples as Robert went on.

"Mother also needs to know your family's guest list. You promised to give it to her last week. She's upset."

Her teeth ground together. "Alright . . . we . . . we can go over the menu again, and I'll figure out the guest list as soon as I can."

"Good, I'll let Mother know. Should I come over? We can go out for dinner," he suggested.

"Uh . . ." Kadie hesitated. She didn't want to go out for dinner, and she really didn't want Robert to know what she was doing. "No," she declined, "no, that's fine. I have a lot to finish up before classes start."

"Are you certain? We could order in?"

She caught her bottom lip between her teeth. She hated to hurt Robert's feelings, but she was excited to discover more about Charlotte and Adelaide.

"No," she reaffirmed, "really. Besides, I've already eaten, and there's no sense driving up here tonight. I'll just be working all evening, and I'll probably have an early night."

"Well, if you're sure . . ."

"Yes, I'm sure."

"Well, good luck with your work then, I guess. I'll call tomorrow and let you know what time Mother wants us."

Kadie groaned silently. "Okay, sounds great. Bye!"

"Good night, Kadie," Robert finished stiffly.

She shut her cell phone and was relieved to end the conversation. She moaned. She wasn't looking forward to an afternoon with "Mother." Kadie felt as if the older woman was constantly looking her nose down at her. She knew Robert's mother didn't approve of her as his choice, and she grimaced. His mother would never believe she was good enough for her *precious* Robert.

She cringed and turned back to her computer. She scrolled down the list. Her lips curved into a smile when she found the correct Adelaide Clarke.

"Adelaide Clarke was born in 1919, in Eureka, Utah. Death . . . "

No date showed for Adelaide's death. *Is she still alive?* Kadie wondered. She searched for another moment. She didn't find any record of death or dates of death given. Her eyebrows rose just as the front door swung open. Kadie turned quickly, nearly toppling out of her chair. She caught sight of Maysha, and she chuckled tersely.

"Good grief! You nearly gave me a heart attack!"

"Really?" Maysha asked. She threw her designer purse onto the table and slumped in a chair. "The restaurant doesn't open until next week—go figure! Aaron had to head back to Provo. Did Robert come over?" she asked, bored.

"No, he called a few minutes ago. He wanted to come over. I think I might have hurt his feelings," she replied with a small smile.

Maysha grinned. "Oh, poor Robert."

Kadie shook her head in exasperation. "Be nice. I'm glad you're home though. You're never going to believe what I've found. Look—" She turned back to her computer, and Maysha stood, coming closer.

Maysha eyed the journal and photo warily and glanced toward the computer screen. "Oh, no! Not this again! I'm not about to—"

"Listen—" Kadie cut in. "I read more of the journal. I was interested. I wanted to know more about her. You know how I get when it comes to genealogy. Charlotte died in 1935—the same year she kept this journal. The last entry was December twenty-third. That means she must have died only a few days later. She was sick, so she may have died of pneumonia . . . " she paused when Maysha picked up the journal. "And this necklace," Kadie went on, "it was a gift from Charlotte to Adelaide. I looked up both Charlotte and Adelaide. I think Adelaide is still alive!"

Ignoring Maysha's incredulous expression, Kadie turned back to her computer and began an advanced search. "Look, it says here that Adelaide Clarke married Fred Moss . . . so she did marry Fred after all." Kadie mused. "She married Fred in 1936. Fred Moss died in

1995 in Tacoma, Washington. If she's still alive, we could find her and . . ."

Maysha stared, open-mouthed, and Kadie laughed before Maysha spoke, "Wow . . . yeah, like I said, this is disturbing. You should have *never* taken that can. We probably brought that girl's ghost home or something. We need to put it back."

"Are you serious? Why?" Kadie gaped.

"Because . . . ," Maysha spluttered. "I . . . I just . . . I just think we should. I don't know why!"

"Think about this, Maysha," Kadie pressed. "If we can find Adelaide . . . if she's still alive, then this belongs to her. This journal could mean the world to her. It was her sister's," she reminded Maysha, taking the journal carefully in her hands.

Maysha groaned, and she reached for a slice of pizza. She took a bite. "So." She chewed, and then swallowed. "How do you suggest we find her? Besides, she'd have to be like . . . one hundred years old or something."

Kadie rolled her eyes. "She was born in 1919, Maysha. She would be eighty-eight. Fred Moss died in Tacoma, Washington. Maybe if we searched in Washington, we would find her." She spun to face her computer and then paused. Where would she look?

"Try Yellow Pages," Maysha suggested sarcastically, her mouth full of pizza.

Kadie shrugged. "We could try the white pages," she murmured and typed *Adelaide Clarke* in the online phone book for Washington State. The search took several moments. No search results were found. Her lips twisted thoughtfully as she typed in *Adelaide Moss*.

"I don't know how you live with your internet," Maysha added dryly. She grabbed another slice of pizza.

"It gets the job done."

"Yeah, in twice as much time."

The connection finally went through, and Kadie smiled when the screen showed Adelaide Moss, Bremerton, Washington, listed. "She's here!" she exclaimed. "But—there's no number, just an address." She scrolled down the list, feeling frustrated at the lack of information available. "Ugh! I don't suppose you have a suggestion for finding unlisted numbers?"

"Nope. Tough noodles." Maysha stood and glared at the coffee can. She shuddered visibly. "Now, will you put those things away? They're freaking me out."

"But this has to be her. Maybe . . ."

"Honestly, Kadie, what are the chances that *this* person," she jerked her finger toward the computer screen, "is even the right old lady? And if it is," she shrugged, "well, write her a letter or something. Better yet, mail her that junk so we can be rid of it." She scowled. "I'm headed to bed. I'm beat after letting you drag me all over the middle of nowhere today. Next week, it's my turn, and we're going *shopping*—at the *Gateway*—all day."

Kadie pulled a face. "How are we even related?"

Maysha grinned. "Tough luck, you owe me."

Kadie stared at the bright computer screen as Maysha turned and disappeared down the hall toward her bedroom. She sighed, thinking about Adelaide Clarke and Charlotte. Could the Adelaide in Bremerton, Washington, really be the same Adelaide?

"It has to be," she whispered.

She could write a letter, but she wished there had been a phone number. Sending a letter just seemed so . . . impersonal. She believed that a sort of connection had developed between herself, Charlotte, and Adelaide. Kadie's mouth twisted thoughtfully. She knew she was being silly. It wasn't usually like her to get overly excited over something like this, but the journal and Charlotte Clarke suddenly seemed very important. She knew she had to get that journal back where it belonged, and it belonged with Adelaide Moss or her family. Sighing again, she turned away from the computer. *I'll write a letter in the morning*, Kadie thought resignedly.

CHAPTER *Three*

The early morning light spilled into her bedroom, rousing Kadie from a restless slumber. She threw the pillow over her face and moaned. She wasn't looking forward to spending a day with Robert and his mother.

"No," she whined and knocked her pillow away.

She squinted against the light as she stumbled to the window to shut the blinds. Glancing at her clock, she moaned again. The clock showed only six-thirty. Maysha wouldn't be awake for hours. Strange dreams had haunted Kadie through the night, and she felt tense and frustrated. The reality of the dream was quickly fading, but Kadie knew she had dreamed of both Charlotte and Adelaide. She glanced at the coffee can sitting on her dresser. Her brow furrowed. Perhaps Maysha was right—maybe they had brought a ghost home after all.

Shaking her head and chuckling at her own paranoia, Kadie got dressed. She pulled on her favorite sport pants and her T-shirt. She pulled her long hair into a pony-tail and then searched for her running shoes. She cringed when she found them buried in the back of her closet, reminding her how long it had been since she last used them.

She tied her shoes and grabbed her portable music player and headphones from off her dresser. Quietly, she left the apartment and headed outside. She needed a good run after a night like she'd had. The morning felt fairly cool, but Kadie knew the sun would soon rise and the temperature in the city would soar. She looked forward to the fall. It would feel nice to have a break from the blistering heat, but she didn't look forward to the sharp sting of winter, either.

She focused on her breathing as she jogged down the sidewalk and turned toward Temple Square. She waved when she passed another jogger. Then she focused on the beautiful spires of the Salt Lake Temple in distance. When she neared the square, she slowed to a walk and gazed past the iron gates to the bountiful array of brightly colored flowers. Decidedly, she strolled onto the square and sat down on a bench to relax, breathing deeply.

She smelled the rich aroma of a thousand flowers, and she inhaled the unique scent, letting it calm her thoughts. She loved the peace she felt while visiting the grounds. The square was quiet and serene, and she gazed about her, taking in the view of the gardens. Her eyes fell on the Family History Library in the distance, and immediately, thoughts of Charlotte and Adelaide came rushing to the surface.

She stood and walked toward the tall building. She knew the building wasn't open, but she still wanted to see it. She peered through the windows and exhaled. She wished she had a better way to contact Adelaide Clarke. Was Adelaide still alive? Had she found the correct information? She believed she had, and a letter just didn't seem adequate. She longed to meet Adelaide face-to-face. She tapped her fingernails against her teeth, frustrated, and turned back toward the entrance. The sun rose higher in the sky, and the heat caused Kadie to sweat uncomfortably.

She glanced back one last time when she reached the gate, and she stopped. A smile touched her full lips as an idea suddenly shaped in her head. She still had more than a week before she had to return to work. What if she tried to find Adelaide? She had an address. That surely was a good start. Kadie started jogging again, hastily making her way back up the hill toward her apartment. She hadn't taken a long road trip in years. *And I've never seen the Northwest*, she justified. A grin spread across her face. If she could just convince Maysha to go along, it would be the perfect end to their summer.

She would be able, she hoped, to meet Adelaide Moss, and if not, she and Maysha would have a great time visiting the coast. She could easily deliver the journal and the pendant. Afterwards, they could spend the rest of the week exploring Washington. Maysha would love Seattle, and Kadie longed to visit the Pacific Coast. *If we hurry, we can leave today*, she thought excitedly. *If we leave this morning, I can avoid another uncomfortable visit with Robert's mother.* She increased her pace and wished that she hadn't taken such a long break from her daily runs. She'd definitely need to get in shape before the new school year started.

She glanced at her watch when she entered the apartment. It was only eight-fifteen. She shut the door and listened for signs telling her Maysha was awake, but the apartment remained quiet, and Kadie knew her sister must still be in bed. She glanced at her watch again, impatient to reveal her plans to Maysha. Her eyes narrowed momentarily as she considered her sister's feelings toward the journal. She knew Maysha didn't want anything to do with Charlotte or Adelaide, but a trip to Seattle was sure to sway her. Kadie's lips curved into a smile, and with determined steps, she hurried down the hall and knocked against Maysha's closed door.

"Go away!" her sister moaned.

Kadie pushed the door open and stepped inside. Maysha lay in bed, the covers pulled over her head, and Kadie grasped a decorative pillow from off the floor to thump her rear end.

"Come on, sleepy head. Wake up!"

"Knock it off," Maysha ordered and sat up. She glared at Kadie, and Kadie grinned, unrepentant.

She sat on the edge of Maysha's bed when Maysha lay down again and pulled the covers back over her head. Kadie pulled the blanket off and laughed. "Hey, I have the best idea," she announced.

"Not another ghost town. I've had it up to my ears with ghosts already." Maysha sat up wearily. "Give me my blanket back!"

Kadie ignored her request. She tossed Maysha's blanket to the floor. "I want to go to Washington. If we left this morning, we could be there by tomorrow, easy. We can find Adelaide Moss and give her the journal, and afterwards you and I can hang out sightseeing for a few days. It will be so fun, and—"

"Whoa—what?" her sister's eyes grew wide. "You want to go to Washington? Today? Okay, who are you? You've never been this spontaneous!"

Kadie leaned closer. "I know, but think about it. You're leaving for school soon and I'm going back to work, and then I'm getting *married*. I've always wanted to visit Washington State, and we have the perfect excuse to go. If this lady really is our Adelaide . . . think what the journal would mean to her. I can't just mail it."

Maysha's mouth fell open. "Are you nuts? We can't just leave . . . today . . . like that."

Kadie shrugged. "Why not?"

"Well—well, I don't know," Maysha sputtered. "What about Robert and Aaron?"

"What about them? We'll only be gone for a week at most, and you'll see Aaron when you're back at school."

"What about Robert? I thought you had plans with him today?" Maysha's eyes narrowed suspiciously.

Kadie frowned. "I do, but he'll get over it. Besides, if I have to think about that wedding for one more day, I'm going to go insane."

" 'That wedding' is your wedding," Maysha responded dryly.

"No," she countered, "that wedding is Robert's *mother's* wedding. Come on. Let's not think about it. Let's just do it. We can pack up and leave in an hour. It'll be fun," she finished with a grin.

She eyed Maysha with a pleading expression as Maysha rolled out of bed. She stretched and yawned. "Alright! Let's do it. But if that old lady isn't the right old lady, you're taking that can and putting it back where you found it—deal?"

* * * * * * *

"The exit should be coming up I think. Yeah . . . pretty sure. You're going to want to merge. Take this exit!" Kadie glanced up and pointed ahead frantically. "Take it, take it!" she yelled.

"Uh . . . aww," Maysha moaned as she cut in front of another vehicle, barely making the exit off the freeway. "I think *you* should drive, because you're *driving me nuts!*"

Kadie calmly laid the map down in her lap. "Do you know how to read a map? I don't think so. If I was driving instead of navigating, we'd be lost."

"We've been lost—twice already," Maysha muttered, giving Kadie a disparaging glance.

Kadie laughed. "Minor navigation problems. I blame the map entirely. Now, just watch for signs that say Bremerton."

"*You* watch for signs that say Bremerton. You're the navigator!"

Kadie pulled a face and laughed. They'd left well before noon the day before and had made good time crossing Idaho and Oregon. It hadn't taken them long to pack and plan their trip. The experience so far felt new and exciting, but Kadie was getting more anxious as the miles passed. Soon they would be in Bremerton, Washington. She wondered if they would really find Adelaide. Maysha was still doubtful.

"Are you sure about this?" Maysha had asked several times before they'd reached Idaho.

Kadie had called Robert once they'd crossed out of Utah into Idaho. She'd thought it best to call him on the road. She was certain he would try to convince her she was insane and demand she turn around. When she decided to call and tell him of her plans, he had been furious. He had called her reckless and insensitive.

"What about Mother?" he'd asked.

His question had infuriated Kadie, and she'd replied curtly, "Tell your mother to decide the menu. She will anyway."

"That's not fair. Mother respects your opinions. You have no idea how this will hurt her. She'd planned lunch today," Robert had haughtily replied.

Kadie was tempted to tell Robert just what he and his mother could do with lunch, but she had clamped her teeth shut. "Robert, I'll see you when I get back. Tell your mother I'm sorry. Goodbye," she'd replied.

"Sounds like he took that well," Maysha had remarked.

"Honestly, I don't know why that man's getting married at all. I'm really beginning to wonder who I'm marrying—him or his mother."

"He's pansy. I've always said it," Maysha had replied. Kadie had frowned, and Maysha laughed. "Hey, I'm just going along with your train of thought."

"I never said he was a pansy."

"You're thinking it," Maysha had taunted.

Kadie shrugged, pushing thoughts of him to the back of her mind. She didn't want to think about Robert today. Soon they would be in Bremerton, and Kadie could almost feel Charlotte's presence. She knew she'd made the right decision to find Adelaide.

"This is beautiful," she remarked, gazing out the Mazda's window.

She had really enjoyed the trip so far. She loved road trips, and the Northwest was just as beautiful as she had imagined. She'd seen only pictures of the West Coast, and she was enthralled with the forests, thick with ferns and moss. They had caught a glimpse of Mount Rainier from the interstate as they headed toward their destination. Now they had just entered Tacoma, and Kadie sat up straighter when she caught sight of the famous Tacoma Narrows Bridge.

When she saw her first glimpse of the ocean, she called, "There's The Sound! I can't believe the size of that bridge."

Maysha blanched, and she slowed the car as they drew near the bridge. Kadie glanced behind them and grimaced. Maysha was holding up traffic, and Kadie smiled when her sister croaked, "I . . . I can't . . . I can't drive across that!"

"It's perfectly fine, you know. Don't be such a coward. You're slowing traffic," Kadie pointed behind them.

Maysha shook her head as they drove closer, and she squealed, "I can't look!"

"Don't close your eyes!" Kadie exclaimed.

"I'm not!" Maysha glared as she drove the car slowly over the bridge.

A horn sounded behind them. Kadie winced. "Just look how beautiful it is," she murmured as they crossed the deep, blue waters.

"*You* look!"

"I am." Kadie replied. Her eyebrows rose as another angry honk sounded behind them. "Would you speed up? You're making everyone mad."

"I don't care."

"You and heights."

Once across the bridge, Maysha pulled over, and Kadie cringed when one driver flashed an obscene gesture. Several more passing cars honked.

Maysha scowled, and Kadie laughed good-naturedly. "Just breathe."

They sat in silence for a moment while her sister took several deep breaths.

"Better?" Kadie asked.

Maysha nodded then smiled sheepishly. She turned the vehicle back onto the road.

Kadie glanced back the way they had come. "I still can't believe I forgot my camera."

"Well, what do you expect when you tear off across the country with absolutely no plans?"

She shrugged. "You have a point."

"How much longer before we reach this old lady's house?"

She glanced at her watch, and her stomach did a little flip. "Not long—only an hour or so."

"And what exactly is our plan? We just find this old lady and tell her 'here—take your dead sister's stuff'?"

Kadie chewed her bottom lip while she contemplated Maysha's questions. She shrugged. "I don't know."

"You don't know? We have to have some sort of plan," Maysha argued.

"I was just going to go along with whatever happens, I guess. I have a good feeling about this, honestly. Think what this journal could mean to Adelaide. This has to be the right person. I just feel it—like it was meant to happen. I mean finding the journal, the necklace, and then the photo? That was no accident. It's almost like Charlotte wants Adelaide to have her journal," she finished.

Maysha eyed her guardedly. "Okay, really, you're weirding me out here. Just . . ." she groaned. "I hope we find this lady soon. I never want to see that stuff again." Maysha shivered. "You brought the address didn't you?"

Kadie grinned and held up a bright orange Post-It note. "Got it."

* * * * * * *

Kadie's stomach turned nervously while Maysha drove the car through the picturesque town of Bremerton. Kadie barely noticed the sights, and she took a deep, calming breath as they searched carefully for the address listed for Adelaide Moss. Soon they left the main part of town behind them and traveled along a water-front road. Kadie caught fleeting glimpses of immaculate homes and the bright, sea-green waters of the Puget Sound through the thick wall of trees that grew alongside the road. Several small lanes turned into the woods, and Kadie believed they were nearing Adelaide's home. She watched the street numbers carefully, then pointed ahead.

"That's it. Take that road there," she directed.

"I can't believe she lives here. She's got to be one rich old lady," Maysha murmured.

Maysha slowed to take the narrow lane that led toward the house. The thick wall of trees on either side of the car darkened the roadway, and Kadie held her breath as she watched the dappled pattern of light filtering through the trees. Again, she hoped that she'd found the right Adelaide Moss. She grasped her stomach when the house came into sight.

Maysha whistled, and Kadie took in the house with wide eyes. Situated on a small precipice overlooking the waters of the Puget Sound, the gray and white house stood three stories high. Its elegant design blended in perfect harmony with the sky and surrounding elements. An immaculate garden framed the circular drive. A giant porch swing swayed in the soft breeze, and potted rhododendrons lined the stairs leading to the front door, adding a splash of vibrant color.

Maysha parked the car in front of the intimidating front porch, and Kadie swallowed hard. Did she really have the right Adelaide? *Well*, she thought, *there's only one way to find out.*

"This lady is loaded. Think she'll give us a nice reward for bringing her that junk?"

"Sick, Maysha. Really sick." Kadie frowned, rolling her eyes as stepped from the car.

The breeze was cool and fresh, and she smelled the spicy scent of the woods and the briny tang of the ocean. She gripped the can in her balmy hands. *This is it, Charlotte*, she mused.

"I was kidding—geeze," Maysha rolled down her window to speak to Kadie.

Pulled from her thoughts, she turned back to face the car. "Aren't you coming?" Maysha shook her head and Kadie scowled. "*Get—out!*" she motioned with agitated hands.

Her sister groaned and slumped from the vehicle. "This is going to be interesting," she commented dryly as they ascended the stone stairs leading to the massive wood door.

Kadie eyed the door bell, a mixture of excitement and nervousness churning in her stomach. "Here goes nothing."

She pushed the button and held her breath when she heard the melodious chimes sounding from within the house. Kadie and Maysha stood for a long moment. Kadie shifted her weight to the opposite leg and rang the bell once more. Again the deep chimes sounded from within.

Maysha shrugged. "Looks like no one's home," she offered just as the door suddenly swung open and she jumped, startled. "Oh, my heck!" she exclaimed, raising a hand to her heart.

"Oh! Hi . . . uh . . . ," Kadie stuttered. She glanced at the young woman standing in the door frame.

"Can I help you?" the woman asked stiffly.

"Yes, I hope so," Kadie began. "Is this the home of Adelaide Moss?" she inquired.

The woman's eyes narrowed and she brushed a long lock of blond hair back from her shoulder. Her blue eyes scanned Kadie's face. "What business do you have with Adelaide Moss?" the woman inquired.

"So she does live here? I'm so glad."

The young woman glanced at Maysha, and then back toward Kadie. "Yes, she does, but how can I help you?" Her eyes were suspicious.

"Well, you see my sister and me—" Kadie went to reply.

"You mean, *you* . . . not me," Maysha cut in.

Kadie frowned at her younger sister and went on, "Okay—*I*—I found something that may belong to her. Can we speak with her, please?"

The young woman shook her head. "No, I'm afraid not. Adelaide isn't well, and she's napping at the moment. She also isn't seeing visitors."

Kadie's shoulders slumped. "Well, we've come a very long way. Is there a time when we can come back? You see, it's very important."

The woman's lips pressed together. "My brother will be home this evening. I suggest you speak with him."

Kadie nodded and smiled. "Thank you," she replied just as a little girl's head popped out from behind the young woman.

Surprised, Kadie stepped back, and the little girl grinned. Her two front teeth were missing and her long, black ponytails swung onto her shoulders as she looked up toward Maysha.

"Who are you?" the girl asked. Maysha stepped back with a frown.

Kadie suppressed a smile. Her sister had never enjoyed children.

"I'm Kadence Reynolds, and this is my sister, Maysha Reynolds," she answered the girl's question.

A frown marred the young woman's face, and she nudged the little girl back inside the house and out of sight. "Go back into the kitchen, Zaza," she replied sternly before she turned and faced them.

"My brother will return this evening. Please come back then." She shut the door.

Kadie and Maysha stood silent on the porch. Kadie heard the sound of the surf and the breeze blowing gently through the trees. She shrugged and glanced at Maysha.

"Well, what now?" Maysha asked.

Kadie smiled, undeterred, and turned to descend the stairs. "We'll come back this evening, like she said. In the mean time, let's go get a motel room and then we'll go sightseeing."

CHAPTER *Four*

$\mathcal{B}$remerton offered an abundant choice of motels near the area, and it didn't take them long to find a cheap place to stay. After checking into their motel, they drove to the nearest gas station, where they filled-up and asked directions to the Evergreen Waterfront Park. They easily found the park, and Kadie glanced around excitedly.

"This is gorgeous," she exclaimed.

Maysha grasped the sack of snacks they'd purchased at the gas station, and they made their way down to the water's edge. They sat on a driftwood log and ate their makeshift lunch. The sounds of the ocean and the park relaxed Kadie. The sun shone brightly, the cool breeze felt wonderful, and she smiled.

"I knew we'd find her," she commented between bites of a chocolate cupcake.

Maysha rolled her eyes as she skimmed a pamphlet she'd found at the gas station. Kadie leaned over to view the map and see what sights Bremerton offered. She pointed to a spot on the map.

"I'd like to go see Harbor-side Fountain Park."

"Later—they have an Arts District, just up from here. That ought to be worth seeing. The boutiques look amazing," Maysha replied wonderingly.

Kadie shrugged and stood, brushing potato chip crumbs from off her lap. She walked to the water's edge and kneeled to let the gentle waves roll across her hand. The water was ice cold, and she shivered slightly. She stood and walked back toward Maysha.

"Let's go see the town. We only have a few hours before we head back to Adelaide's house," Kadie spoke.

Maysha sighed and popped another chip in her mouth. "You sure about this?" she asked with her mouth full. "We didn't exactly get a very warm welcome," she reminded Kadie.

Kadie nodded, undaunted. "I'm sure. It has to be her, and I need to see the journal back where it belongs."

"It belongs in a hole in the ground, right where you found it. You should have left it there," Maysha replied.

The corners of Kadie's mouth quirked. "It's fine. Try to be a bit more optimistic."

"You have enough optimism for the both of us. I can't wait to get rid of that journal."

* * * * * * *

They spent the remainder of the afternoon exploring Bremerton, and when six o'clock rolled around, Kadie felt her tension mount. Would she get the chance to meet Adelaide? She wondered what the young woman's brother was like. Would he give her a chance to explain? Her stomach rolled uncomfortably as Maysha drove the little Mazda down the road toward Adelaide's home.

"You'll come up with me again, right? You're with me on this?" Kadie asked when Maysha pulled the car into the drive.

"Aren't I always?"

They again ascended the large stone steps, and Kadie chewed her bottom lip. She rang the doorbell. The familiar tune sounded through the house, and she held her breath expectantly. The door swung wide and she smiled a greeting to the same young woman. The woman's smile quickly turned to a frown. She scowled openly.

"Hi," Kadie spoke. "Is your brother or his wife home? You said to come back later."

The woman nodded curtly. "My brother isn't married. Wait here," she replied and shut the door.

Maysha glanced at Kadie and her eyebrows rose. "Very friendly," Maysha remarked sarcastically.

Kadie shrugged then turned to face the door when the sound of heavy footfalls drew closer. The door swung open, and she peered up at the tall man who stood framed in the doorway. His styled hair was thick and dark, and a slight scowl marred his tanned, vaguely handsome face.

"Can I help you?" he asked.

Kadie hesitated before she answered, "My name is Kadence Reynolds. This is my sister, Maysha."

"Logan Matthews," he introduced himself. "Kadence and Maysha Reynolds?" he reaffirmed.

Maysha nodded and grinned. "Our mother was going through her Harlequin Romance stage when we were born."

Logan's mouth quirked and Kadie laughed nervously before she addressed him. "People call me Kadie." She shrugged then went on, "But we've come from Utah to meet Adelaide Moss. We've found something that we hope belongs to her."

Logan Matthews eyebrows rose skeptically. "Utah? What have you found exactly?"

Kadie held up the old coffee can. "It's a long story," she began, "you see we were wondering if perhaps Adelaide had a sister named Charlotte? We—"

"How do you know that?" He eyed her suspiciously and Kadie rushed to explain.

"Well, you see my sister and I—"

"*You*—you mean *you*!" Maysha cut in.

Kadie frowned and rolled her eyes. "Okay, I mean I—I was exploring an old ghost town in Utah called Eureka. I was walking through an old foundation. Some of the flooring was still in place, and my foot fell through a hole in the floor. I discovered this can inside the hole. Inside the can, I found a diary that belonged to Charlotte Clarke. I haven't read the entire journal, but the entries begin and end in 1935. Charlotte talks about her twin sister, Adelaide . . . "

She paused when she noticed his eyes had grown wide with surprise. Feeling more hopeful, she continued, "There was also a necklace inside the can. Later that day, we found this photo in an antique store in town."

She stopped to pull the old photograph from the paper bag. She handed it to Logan, and he accepted it guardedly.

"The chick in the picture is wearing the same necklace that Kadie found," Maysha added while he studied the photograph with narrowed eyes.

"We knew then that this journal must have belonged to Charlotte Clarke. I did some research on Charlotte and Adelaide Clarke, and I was able to trace Adelaide Moss here," Kadie finished.

She held her breath when Logan looked up from the picture and his eyes met hers. "You found this journal in that can—in an old foundation?" he asked.

Kadie nodded and Maysha laughed. "It's an odd hobby my sister has. She likes old things. She's a real history geek."

"I know it sounds unbelievable. I'm a Utah history teacher. I teach at a junior high in Salt Lake. I've spent all summer exploring ghost towns. Eureka was my last stop." She pulled the lid off the coffee can and reached in to grab the journal. "I was amazed to find this." She handed the journal to Logan. "It's still in excellent condition considering how many years it's been in this can."

Logan turned the journal around in his large, dark hands before he opened it carefully. Kadie reached in for the pendant. She unwound the fabric and handed the pendant to Logan. "See—it's the same," she murmured.

He studied the charm for a moment before he looked at her. "You and your sister drove all the way here—to give this to Adelaide?"

"All we had was an address. I . . . well, it was a bit reckless, but a letter didn't seem adequate. I wanted to give her these things in person. I felt it was important for her to have them. This journal belongs with your family," Kadie concluded.

Logan's eyes narrowed. He remained silent while he studied her. She blushed under his close scrutiny. She felt like a strange organism under a microscope, and she squirmed uncomfortably.

"You have to understand," he began, "my grandmother is quite ill. Her health is failing. I don't want to upset her, and I don't want her overly excited. I'll see to it that she gets these. I'm sure you understand," he finished.

Kadie's shoulders fell and she tried hard to hide her sudden, overwhelming disappointment. "Oh . . . yes, of course. I understand," she mumbled.

She handed the can and the lid to Logan and watched despondently while he replaced the journal and necklace inside. He tucked the photo under his arm and shook Kadie's hand.

"Thank you. This will mean a lot to her. How long do you plan to stay in town?" he asked.

"We have a motel here in town for the night. Tomorrow . . . well, we hadn't really thought that far ahead. Like I said, it was kind of a spur-of-the-moment trip."

"I see," Logan responded. "I'll see that she gets this, and if you'll write down your name and address, I'll see that you are fully compensated for your time and trip expenses."

Kadie's mouth fell open and she was quick to reply, "No! Oh—no. We didn't come out here expecting a reward or compensation. I simply wanted Adelaide to have these things. The diary and pendant belong to her."

Again he regarded her carefully. "I see," he murmured. "Well, thank you. This will mean a great deal to her." He nodded. "Have a good night."

Kadie smiled and glanced at Maysha. Their eyes met and Maysha shrugged.

"Good night," Kadie replied. She turned to descend the stairs.

The large door shut behind her and she exhaled noisily. Disappointment weighed heavy as they returned to the car and drove away from the house.

"Thank goodness that's over," her sister murmured when they returned to town. She turned the Mazda in the direction of their motel.

"Yeah," Kadie replied dispassionately.

Maysha glanced at Kadie. "What did you expect? Oh, come on!"

Kadie's shoulders slumped. "I wanted to meet her. I wanted to see her in person. I just felt like . . . like . . . I don't know." She stopped and sighed.

"Seriously? Okay, whatever, Kadie. Personally, I'm glad to be rid of that stuff. You've done nothing but obsess over those things since you've found them. The whole situation was just—"

"Creepy. I know," Kadie finished for her.

* * * * * * *

Back at the motel, Kadie eyed her disappointed reflection in the misty bathroom mirror. She reached for her toothbrush just as Maysha popped her head around the corner, her image appearing in the mirror next to Kadie's.

"You can't seriously be getting ready for bed. I'm starving! Let's order pizza and watch a movie," she suggested.

Kadie couldn't help but smile. She felt exhausted after the day's events, but a movie and pizza with her sister sounded great. She wrapped a towel around her wet hair and smeared fade cream across her face before she left the bathroom. She grabbed a local magazine from off the nightstand and then moved to sit on the bed. She flipped through the tourism magazine while Maysha ordered a large pizza and a two-liter of soda.

"Why don't we go into Seattle tomorrow?" Kadie suggested when Maysha finished ordering the pizza. "We can spend the day there and find a motel in the city."

"Sounds great," Maysha agreed, coming to sit next to Kadie on the large bed.

Maysha flipped through the channels on the small television and they watched the last half of a sitcom while they waited for their pizza to arrive. Soon, a knock sounded against the door, and Kadie rushed to get her wallet before she swung the door open wide. She took a quick step back, startled, when her eyes met Logan Matthews.

"Um . . . " Kadie stammered. "Hi . . . ?" Her eyes widened.

Logan nodded. "I'm sorry to come by so late."

His eyes traveled the length of her pajama-clad body, and she read the humor in his expression when his gaze fell on the liberal amount of fade cream she had smeared across her face. Kadie's lips parted and her cheeks grew red.

"We were . . . uh . . . " She raised a self-conscious hand to the towel still wrapped about her head. "Come in?"

"Hi, again. Do you want to come in?" Maysha repeated. Logan glanced past Kadie to wave at her sister.

"No thanks. I stopped by to invite you back to the house tomorrow morning. Adelaide insisted on seeing you," Logan replied.

Stunned, Kadie asked, "How did you find us?"

"I drove past every motel and hotel in Bremerton," he replied, with a lopsided grin. "I found your vehicle, but I'm afraid that I may have bothered a few of your neighbors trying to find the right room."

"Adelaide wants to see us?" Kadie felt her excitement growing.

Logan nodded. "Like I said, I'm sorry to barge in on you so late, but she insisted I find you before you had a chance to leave town."

Forgetting her embarrassment over her unusual appearance, Kadie's eyes widened. "I'm so glad! We'd love to come!"

He nodded and his eyes rested on the lopsided towel wrapped around her head. His mouth quirked. "Tomorrow morning would be best. She gets very tired in the afternoon. Would nine-o'clock work for you?"

"Yes, that would be great," Kadie answered.

"Good! I'll see you tomorrow morning then." He waved and turned away.

Kadie smiled openly and called, "Thank you, Mr. Matthews."

Logan paused. He turned back toward Kadie. "Please, call me Logan."

He was about to turn away when the pizza delivery car pulled into the crowded parking lot with an ear-splitting screech. Kadie watched as a teenage boy jumped out of a beat-up vehicle, and he eyed Logan and Kadie.

"Hey, did someone order a pizza?" he asked.

Kadie raised her hand. "That would be me."

She reached for her wallet just as Logan placed a hand on the boy's arm. "How much?" he asked.

"Twenty dollars and thirty-five cents."

Kadie watched mutely while Logan pulled two twenty-dollar bills from his wallet. He handed the money to the boy. The boy grinned knowingly before passing the pizza to Kadie.

"You didn't have to do that," she protested.

Logan waved. "My pleasure. See you tomorrow." He turned away and walked to his car. He waved one last time just before he slid behind the wheel, and she watched as the BMW sped out of the parking lot and disappeared down the road.

She stepped back into the room and slowly shut the door. "That was unexpected," she muttered.

Maysha nodded. "Yeah, did he pay for the pizza?" Kadie nodded. "Great! That's twenty less that I owe you now."

Kadie shook her head, but smiled as she reached for a wide slice of pizza. Tomorrow she'd finally get to meet Adelaide Clarke.

CHAPTER *Five*

*K*adie eyed her appearance critically while she finished curling her long, auburn hair. She had left her hair hanging loose. Its thick length spilled down across her shoulders, and she fleetingly wondered if she should have pulled it up considering Washington's reputation for rain. She walked into the bedroom and moved the curtain aside. The sun shone in a cloudless sky. She stepped to the table and sat down to apply a touch of makeup. Maysha was still in the bathroom curling her hair, and it was already eight-o'clock. Kadie's stomach clenched when she thought of how close she was to meeting Adelaide. *And*, she mused, *seeing Logan Matthews again*. She finished her makeup and glanced at the clock once again.

"I'm going to grab a bite of breakfast from the lobby," Kadie called. "Do you want me to get you anything?"

Maysha's head popped out of the bathroom. "Yeah," she answered, "grab me a muffin or something, will ya?"

"Sure," Kadie replied as she stepped outside and shut the door.

She breathed in the cool air and the unusual smell of the Sound. Her nose wrinkled. The smell, she would have to get used to, but she found she enjoyed Washington. *I wonder if Utah history teachers are in demand here*, she thought with a smile. She wouldn't mind the change.

Suddenly, she remembered Robert, and her smile faltered. He'd never consider leaving Utah and his mother. She frowned as she walked into the lobby, and as if on cue, her phone rang. Pulling her cell from her purse, she checked the caller ID. She cringed when she saw it was Robert. *What is the matter with me? I'm marrying him*, she reminded herself as she flipped the phone open.

"Hello, Rob," she answered with forced cheerfulness.

"Kadie, you know how I hate being called Rob," he scolded, and Kadie frowned.

"Sorry, Robert." She pulled a face at the phone. Then feeling somewhat juvenile, she repeated, "I'm sorry, I forgot."

"You didn't call last night. I was beginning to worry." He did sound concerned.

"Really, I forgot. We were so tired after all that driving. We just called it an early night," she explained.

"And this wild goose chase you're on—did you find what you're looking for?" he asked, sounding ever-more petulant.

"Yes, as a matter of fact, I did. We found Adelaide Moss. Maysha and I are going to meet with her in another hour or so."

"Really? Well, I suppose congratulations are in order then," he replied stiffly.

"Robert," Kadie began then paused. She felt reluctant to tell him anything more concerning Adelaide, so instead she forced herself to ask, "How is your mother?"

"She's beside herself trying to plan the luncheon. I wish you had taken the time to meet with her before you set off on this ridiculous venture of yours," he admonished.

Kadie bit her tongue, trying hard to keep back her angry retort. She closed her eyes and silently counted to ten.

"Kadie?"

"I'm here," she breathed. "I am sorry, but in all honesty, the wedding isn't until December. I'm sure your mom will have everything sorted out by then."

"Nevertheless—"

"Yes, well, nevertheless," she cut him off. "Listen, I really need to go. I . . . I'll call you later, okay?"

"I have meetings until seven."

"Alright—I'll talk to you when I can then," she sighed. She hated when they argued.

"Really, Kadie, you're just not acting like yourself. I'm concerned," he replied with an anger-edged voice.

Kadie scowled openly. "I'm . . . I'll call later. Goodbye." Without waiting for his reply, she shut her cell phone.

She raised a hand to her temple and rubbed her head absently. *Why am I marrying him?* She asked herself. She did love him, didn't she? She did, but was it the sort of love that could endure a lifetime of marriage? She frowned. She didn't have time to sort through her muddled thoughts. She needed to grab a quick bite of breakfast then rush Maysha. The last thing she wanted was to be late for her meeting with Adelaide Moss.

* * * * * * *

"Well, here we go again," Maysha complained when she and Kadie reached Adelaide's front door.

Kadie chuckled and rang the doorbell. They waited only a moment before the large door swung wide, and Logan's sister greeted Kadie and Maysha with a smile.

"Hi, come on in. I'm Elizabeth Matthews. Call me Beth." She shook their hands before she stepped back to let them enter.

Kadie returned her greeting with a warm smile, and Maysha raised her eyebrows irreverently. Kadie gave her sister a sharp look and replied, "Thank you for letting us come. Logan—"

"I know," Beth cut in with a smile. "I'm sorry about yesterday. I hope I didn't seem rude. We just don't like Grandma to be disturbed."

"I understand," Kadie responded.

Her gaze took in the massive house. A huge, wood-and-steel staircase led to the upper floors. The flooring was a beautiful hard wood, and she saw a spacious kitchen and living area beyond the staircase. The house was bright with sunlight that spilled into the rooms from several large windows that faced the ocean, and the decorations were sparse but elegant.

"Wow," Maysha openly admired the house.

"Your home is beautiful," Kadie added.

"Oh, thank you. This is my brother's house," Beth replied just as the same little girl appeared in the spacious hallway.

She bounded toward them, her pigtails swinging and a grin spread across her face. Instinctively, Kadie smiled. The little girl was charming.

"Hi, I'm Zaza," the girl spoke as she approached. She hid behind Beth's leg and peeked curiously at Kadie.

"Hello, " Kadie returned with a smile. She glanced toward Beth. "You're daughter is adorable."

"Oh," Beth shook her head and placed a hand on the girl's head. "No, I'm her aunt. Zahara is Logan's daughter. We call her Zaza for short," she explained.

Kadie's lips parted, and then suddenly she jumped when Logan's deep voice sounded directly above them.

"I'm glad you're here."

Kadie's eyes shot toward the staircase, and she caught her breath as he descended toward them. His dark eyes fell on hers and again an unfamiliar blush stole up her neck. *Get a hold of yourself,* she scolded privately.

He reached the entry way and greeted them with a slight smile and a nod before he directed his attention to Zaza. "Go into the kitchen. You need to finish your breakfast." He gave the little girl a stern look, but she stepped forward quickly, grasping his large hand in hers.

"But, Daddy—" she began.

Logan shook his head. "Do as you're told, Zaza. Go on."

Zaza's grin faded and her thin shoulders slumped as she turned and sulked back toward the kitchen.

He watched his daughter return to the kitchen table before he turned to face them. "My grandma will be glad to see you. She's unable to walk and she's feeling very weak this morning, but if you'll follow me, I'll show you to her room."

He turned and they followed him up the impressive staircase in silence. The second floor was just as grand as the first, with large windows that looked out toward a grand expanse of lawn. The grass was green and soft and the ocean lay just beyond a narrow strip of sandy beach. Kadie caught her breath at the sight.

"It's beautiful here," she murmured.

Logan agreed with a slight nod of his head, and Kadie glanced around curiously when he led them down a wide hallway. Within moments, they entered a small sitting room with a bedroom off toward the right.

He turned into the bedroom and Kadie followed, feeling nervous. What was Adelaide like? Logan paused in the bedroom's entryway and knocked against the door frame. He glanced inside just as a soft voice called, "Come in."

He stepped to the side and ushered Kadie and Maysha into the room. The room was spacious but crowded with various pieces of medical equipment, and Kadie heard the soft whir of an oxygen concentrator. Her eyes fell immediately to the center of the room, where a frail old woman lay in a hospital-style bed. She was sitting, propped upright by several large pillows, and her long, white hair spilled down across her shoulders. The pendant lay against Adelaide's chest. Kadie hesitated and the woman smiled, beckoning Kadie with a wave of her frail hand. Kadie's eyes traveled around the bedroom and her gaze fell on the nightstand where the familiar coffee can sat. The journal lay open next to the photograph, and Kadie smiled shyly before she stepped closer.

Logan approached the bedside and placed a kiss on Adelaide's forehead. "I've brought some visitors." His eyes met Kadie's, and he smiled.

"Mrs. Moss," Kadie greeted.

"Please, come closer. I'm so happy to meet you," Adelaide spoke. Her voice was whispery and weak.

Kadie stepped toward the bed, and Logan moved back against the wall to make more space for her. She glanced back toward Maysha and frowned when her sister hovered near the door. She sighed and turned her attention back to Adelaide.

"I'm happy to meet you too, Mrs. Moss," Kadie replied.

Adelaide held out a frail hand, and with a smile, Kadie placed her hand in Adelaide's. Immediately Kadie felt a sense of peace and an instantaneous kinship. She smiled into the older woman's eyes.

Adelaide glanced past Kadie and beckoned toward Maysha. "Come in, dear."

Maysha moved hesitantly behind Kadie, and Kadie gave her sister an encouraging smile.

"So, Logan tells me that you two discovered Charlotte's and my secret hiding hole." Adelaide smiled at Maysha.

"No—Kadie did," she replied almost accusingly.

Kadie caught a glimpse of Logan's reflection in the mirror hanging on the far wall. He was laughing silently.

"I did. I sort of fell into it." She shrugged sheepishly.

"I imagine you must have." Adelaide laughed. "Please sit down." Adelaide released Kadie's hand and motioned toward a soft armchair next to the bed. "And bring that extra chair around, Logan," she directed.

Logan pushed away from the wall to grab a chair from the opposite end the room. He carried it close to Adelaide's bed, and Kadie smiled her thanks.

"Hand me that book, please." Adelaide pointed to the journal and Kadie reached for it, carefully handing the book to Adelaide. "I can't begin to tell you what this means to me. Imagine—for it to have survived all these years." Adelaide shook her head, amazed. "Logan spent all night reading to me. I felt as though Charlotte were in the room with me, laughing and crying together as we once had as girls. Oh, how I've missed her—how I've missed them all." She paused and her eyes shone with unshed tears. "Alvin, Ruthie . . . baby Ruth . . . Mama and Papa."

Adelaide's eyes fell on Kadie, and she felt surprised at how vibrantly blue they were. Kadie smiled, but remained silent.

"Have you read this?" Adelaide asked.

"Some," Kadie admitted, "but not all."

The frail woman nodded slowly. "Charlotte's last entry—December, twenty-third—that's a date I have never forgotten. That was the night of the fire."

Fire? Kadie inhaled sharply. *So the fire had destroyed the home.* She shivered and caught Maysha's cutting glance. Goosebumps rose on Kadie's arms as she remembered the ruin. She had seen the charred wood and smelled the burned, decaying timbers. She held her breath as Adelaide went on.

"They didn't make it out. Not one—Papa, Mama, Alvin, Ruthie, and Charlotte—dear Charlotte," she said the names reverently.

Kadie's eyes broadened. *They'd died?* Tears stung the rim of her eyes. *All of them?* Her lips parted and she gasped.

"The house was engulfed in flames before anyone noticed. By then it was too late. They were gone. I returned home from the road show and my family was gone—just like that." Adelaide dabbed at a tear that slid down her deeply wrinkled cheek, and Kadie could no longer keep her own tears in check. She wiped at a fat tear when Adelaide continued.

"All the bodies were accounted for, but not Charlotte's. They never found her body. They searched the ruins for days. They searched the hills, the town, and even the old mine shafts, but they never found her. I waited for days, praying and hoping she'd return. But there was no word, no sign of her body, no indication . . . it was as if she disappeared into thin air. People whispered that Charlotte set that terrible fire and ran away. Terrible rumors—the horrible things people said. I can still hear them. My sister, my very best friend, was gone—without a trace. They listed her as a casualty of the fire in the end."

A shiver stole up Kadie's back. "Adelaide . . . ." she spoke.

The elderly woman smiled knowingly and patted her hand before she pointed firmly at the journal sitting on her lap. "My sister did not run away and I have never believed she started that fire. No one knows what happened that night. Papa and Mama were always so careful with the stove. Mama checked it every night—always so careful . . ." Adelaide's voice trembled. She closed her eyes.

"Adelaide, I'm so sorry," Kadie murmured. The older woman's lips twitched, but she did not open her eyes.

Kadie glanced at Logan. He smiled a little, and Kadie watched as he leaned over Adelaide and took the journal from her lap. He turned the journal around in his dark hands before he placed it back onto the nightstand. He spoke, "She needs her rest."

Kadie stood. "Is she . . . ?" she whispered, and Logan nodded.

"She's asleep. She tends to nod off quickly." He tapped the journal with his finger absently before he moved toward the door.

They followed him into the sitting room, but Kadie paused in the doorway. She glanced back toward Adelaide. How tragic, to find yourself orphaned as Adelaide had. She'd lost everything and everyone she loved. Never understanding or knowing what really happened would be such a terrible burden.

Logan cleared his throat, and she turned to face him as he spoke. "She tends to sleep for several hours at a time. However, I'm certain when she wakes up, she'll want to see you again. Perhaps you could stay for lunch or if you don't mind, you could come back later this afternoon?"

Kadie glanced at her sister.

Maysha shook her head. "No," she mouthed the word.

Kadie's eyebrows shot up in amusement before she answered. "We don't mind at all. I've been intrigued with Adelaide and Charlotte since we found the journal—"

"More like obsessed," Maysha cut in.

Kadie gave her sister a warning look and finished, "I would love to stay and visit with Adelaide a while longer."

Logan nodded thoughtfully. "Stay for lunch—I know Beth is anxious to visit with you. She doesn't get out much."

Kadie's eyes found Maysha's. She was shaking her head and scowling behind Logan's back. She knew her sister didn't want to stay. Kadie was sure Maysha would much rather eat at a café in town and spend the day shopping as they had planned, but Kadie felt very reluctant to leave. They'd come so far to meet Adelaide, and they were finally here. She couldn't leave yet.

Spending a day with an ailing woman and her family won't kill Maysha, she justified before she answered Logan. "We'd love to stay for lunch," she replied and cringed when she caught sight of Maysha's enraged expression.

Kadie's face turned pleading as they turned to follow Logan down the stairs.

"What—are—you . . . ." Maysha whispered between clenched teeth and Kadie jabbed her in the ribs as they walked next to each other toward the kitchen.

"Shhh!" she cautioned and smiled when Beth came out of the kitchen to greet Logan.

"You're joining us for lunch then?" Beth asked.

"Yes, we'd love to."

They entered the spacious kitchen and dining area, and like the rest of the home, the kitchen was striking, with elaborate design elements integrated to give it an awe-inspiring yet elegant look. Immense sliding-glass doors led outside to a red brick porch, and the immaculate yard stretched out to the sea. Zaza, who was playing on the grass, caught sight of the adults, and she skipped across the yard and into the kitchen.

"Daddy!" she called and threw herself into Logan's strong arms.

Logan caught her to him then tapped the end of her nose playfully. "Have you introduced yourself to our guests, princess?"

Zaza nodded. "Yes, sir, that's Kadence and that's Maysa," she answered.

"*Maysha*," Maysha corrected with a slight scowl.

Kadie smiled at the sweet girl. "You can call me Kadie, if you like. You have a lovely house, Zahara, and a very nice family."

"You can call me Zaza! You wanna see my room?" The little girl pushed out of Logan's arms and grabbed onto Kadie's hand.

"Not now. Aunt Beth has lunch ready, and Kadence and her sister are going to eat with us. Go on and wash up," Logan replied.

"You're going to stay? Yay!" Zaza called as she rushed out of the kitchen and disappeared around a corner.

Kadie laughed and caught Logan's eye. He watched her curiously, and again she felt a quick blush rise to her cheeks. Feeling unnaturally shy, she smiled then cringed. *Stop being so foolish*, she chided. When Logan turned toward the stove, Kadie saw Maysha's dour expression. Kadie rolled her eyes and faced the glass door to peer out at the scene beyond. She half listened while Logan and Beth conversed with one another, and her thoughts drifted to Adelaide.

She was not normally a superstitious person. She didn't believe in ghosts, but Kadie believed Charlotte wanted her to find that journal, hidden and preserved all those years in the charred remains of the home. The thought sent a chill down her spine, and she could clearly remember the haunted feeling she had experienced while standing in the ruins.

The fire had claimed every member of Adelaide's family, but had Charlotte died in the fire? Why had Charlotte's body never been found? She shivered again as she remembered the moment when she'd stepped across the burned timbers. She'd touched the charred stone, had smelled the musty, acrid scent of burned wood. She'd stood within the remains of a home that had once known love, but had ended in tragedy. What had caused the fire?

Her lips twisted ruefully, and she forced her thoughts back to the present. She watched as the waves of the Puget Sound lapped at the sandy stretch of beach. Large driftwood logs lay scattered haphazardly along the coast line, and there were several boats on the water.

A smile touched her lips when she caught sight of a pelican perched on a log. Several different shore birds skittered along the sand.

"The view is amazing," she whispered.

Logan moved across the kitchen, and his shoes sounded against the stone-tiled floor. He moved next to her, and she caught her breath abruptly. Logan Matthews definitely caused a strange mix of emotions. Her stomach knotted, and she groaned. *You're acting like a child*, she reproached. She had just met the man, yet she was behaving like a love-drunk teenager. *Besides*, she reminded herself, *I'm supposed to be madly in love with Robert. I'm getting married in four months, for heaven sake's.*

"I've always enjoyed the view," Beth spoke from across the kitchen, and Kadie turned to face her. She stood at a massive gas stove, stirring a pot on the flames.

"Can I help?" Kadie asked.

"Oh, no, it's ready, I'll just set the table," Beth replied.

Kadie turned toward the table and smiled at Maysha, who sat slumped in a kitchen chair, a dour expression on her face. Zaza had returned and was eagerly pulling her crayons and coloring books toward Maysha. Kadie's smile broadened. Her sister had never tolerated children well.

CHAPTER *Six*

*B*eth served a light lunch, and Kadie enjoyed the pasta and red sauce immensely. Zaza had insisted on sitting next to Maysha, and Kadie laughed at the sight of the little girl's excited expression as she chattered non-stop.

"*Maysa* is a weird name, but so is Zahara. I'm in first-grade, and the girl who sits next to me—she's mean. Her name's Brittany. She makes fun of me and calls me Sahara—like the desert! I'm not a desert! I like my teacher though. Her name is Miss Tully! Oh, hey . . . ," Zaza paused and faced Kadie.

Kadie laughed as she watched Zaza's animated face. "Yes?" she encouraged.

Zaza took a breath and then went on quickly, "Daddy says you're a teacher. He says you teach at Moose Ridge School." She giggled. "That's a funny name for a school."

"I do teach at Moose Ridge," she answered, and her mouth twisted. She was certain she hadn't told Logan where she taught school.

Logan suddenly coughed and cleared his throat. "Well, yes— Zaza, why don't you go play outside for a while?"

The little girl's brow knit, confused and then she frowned. "But . . . ?"

"Please?" he cut in.

With a scowl, Zaza gathered her coloring books into her skinny arms. "Humph." She stomped her bare feet as she marched toward the sliding glass door. She jerked the door open and stepped outside before she slumped into a chair near the porch.

Kadie caught Logan's eye and he smiled, embarrassed. "I did check. I'm sorry. I was . . ." He paused, "I was curious and I needed to make sure everything was on the up-and-up. Forgive me," he finished.

She shrugged. "That's understandable."

"Yeah, I'd say. I mean how often do two crazy women show up on your doorstep with a can of stuff that belonged to your dead great-aunt," Maysha chimed in.

Beth chuckled. "I have to admit—it was a little bewildering."

"Well, who else but my sister finds a ghost? I swear, the whole situation is just creepy," she continued.

"Maysha . . . ." Kadie admonished, embarrassed.

"I have to admit, I'm with Maysha on this. I had goose-bumps when Logan told me. How did you find the journal again?" Beth inquired.

"I was exploring the foundation of the house. There are still a few walls standing, and I noticed there had been a fire, but I assumed the fire had burned the house down after it had been abandoned. My foot fell through the floor. That's when I noticed the can in the hole."

"I can't believe it survived the fire and all these years." Beth paused and added, "Like I said, I agree with Maysha. It's creepy. The fire and Aunt Charlotte's disappearance has always been such a mystery. It's haunted Grandma all her life. She's talked about Aunt Charlotte for as long as I can remember. All the family photos were destroyed in the fire. I can't believe you stumbled on that picture the way you did. That photograph must have been taken only days before the fire. I've never seen Grandma react the way she did when we handed her that picture and Aunt Charlotte's possessions. It was like we had brought her sister back from the dead. The likeness of the sisters is amazing." Beth shivered as she finished.

Kadie nodded and Logan spoke, "Well, all talk of ghosts aside, I have to say, it is amazing." He turned to face her. "Did you happen to read that last entry?"

"Yes, I did," she answered. "Although at the time, I hadn't realized that Charlotte died in a fire. What a terrible tragedy. I discovered Charlotte died in 1935, but I assumed she died of pneumonia."

Logan nodded, his expression thoughtful. "You read about the argument between Adelaide's father and Mr. Jukes?"

Kadie nodded and Logan went on, "I found that interesting. Grandma has mentioned Adam Jukes through the years—here and there. He was a senator living in Seattle. The Jukes family moved to Seattle several years after Grandma and Grandpa settled here. That's why I remembered the name. Grandpa was really put out when Adam Jukes was elected to the senate. Apparently Adam Jukes' father was also a senator in Utah. His father was elected to the Utah State Senate in 1936. I've done a bit of research this morning, and I found that Adam Jukes' sons and his grandsons are all heavily involved in politics. It seems the Jukes are quite a prominent family."

"So what are you saying, Logan?" Beth asked.

Logan shrugged. "Nothing really, I just found it interesting."

* * * * * * *

Logan sat in silence, staring out at the moon's distorted reflection across the water. The narrow strip of beach looked almost ethereal in the moonlight. Several lights shimmered in the distance as fishing boats came into port. He felt tempted to sneak away from the house for a quick swim. The night was the sort of perfect summer night that beckoned him. He loved swimming in the frigid waters of the Puget Sound. He'd been drawn to the water ever since he, his younger brother, Jace, and Beth had moved to the Pacific Northwest to live with his grandparents following the death of their parents.

He leaned back in his chair, remembering the many years that had passed since he'd first come to live with Adelaide and Fred. He'd been sixteen, the same age Adelaide had been when she'd lost her own family. When Logan lost his parents, he'd felt as though he'd lost everything. However, he'd still had Jace and Beth. Adelaide had lost everyone. She'd married Fred soon after the fire, but her loneliness and grief would have been overwhelming. Logan had been the oldest, but Beth and Jace had really helped pull him through that first, tough year. He couldn't imagine what it would have been like if he'd lost his entire family as Adelaide had.

His thoughts turned to Adelaide, laying so frail and weak just down the hall. It was hard to see her fading away. She'd done her very best to give him and his siblings a secure life. He knew raising three teenagers hadn't been easy for her and Fred. Beth had been twelve at the time, and Jace, fifteen. Logan had used his grief over losing his parents as an excuse to rebel against the values he'd been taught and he knew he hadn't made his grandparent's life very easy. Unfortunately, Jace had been only too eager to follow his bad example, but Adelaide had been patient and understanding, and Fred had been stern but kind. They'd done a remarkable job raising him and his siblings, and now, as an adult, he couldn't be more grateful. His grandparents had helped push him through high school and then college, and they'd supported and encouraged him through the long years spent in law school.

Jace had gone on to become a successful accountant in New York, and Beth . . . well—Logan owed Beth for many lost years. She'd taken time from college to help care for their ailing grandfather, while he and Jace finished grad school. She'd just returned to school when Adelaide had taken a turn for the worse, and at the time, he'd been struggling with a failing marriage and a newborn daughter.

Jace had been newly married, and was just starting a family and a new career in upstate New York. So, once again, Beth had put her life on hold to help care for their grandmother. Once Logan's divorce was out of the way, he'd purchased this house and moved Adelaide and Beth in. On the outside, it looked to be a great act of selflessness; moving his ailing grandmother and unmarried sister into such a grand home, but Logan knew he'd had his own selfish motives.

Beth had been a miracle, helping him raise Zaza. He'd been clueless and scared to death, wondering how to raise an infant daughter and still manage to keep his career as a criminal defense lawyer intact. He had to work long, odd hours. Without his sister . . . well, he didn't know where he'd be without her.

He stood and stretched his broad shoulders then turned when he heard Beth's soft footsteps on the stairs. She approached his office door and he waited to hear the familiar quiet knock.

"Come in," he called.

"Is Zaza in bed?" she asked, stepping into the office.

She carried two cups of steaming herbal tea, and she handed one to Logan. He caught the crisp, familiar scent of peppermint. He had always enjoyed Beth's peppermint tea. He took a sip before he nodded. "Yes, it took a while and a few extra books. I'm afraid she has ghosts on her mind." He laughed quietly and took another sip of his drink.

"She's not the only one," Beth admitted. "What do you think of all this? I have to admit, it's left me a bit unsettled."

"I don't believe in ghosts." He grinned. "However, I . . . well, it is hard to explain. I had my doubts about those two women at first, but I can't help feeling amazed. Finding that journal . . . " He paused. "That last entry, the night of the fire, maybe it's the lawyer in me, but I can't seem to shake the feeling the fire was no accident. I've always assumed Aunt Charlotte died in the fire, but now I don't know. It's strange, but I can't help wondering what really happened that night."

Beth laughed nervously. "It isn't like you to dwell on something like this, but I did wonder myself. The fire was never explained and Aunt Charlotte's body was never found."

He nodded. A slight smile touched his lips. "Grandpa had a serious aversion to Senator Jukes. I remember him saying over the years, 'Ain't it bad enough Utah had to elect a Jukes idiot? Now Washington has to follow suit.'" Logan laughed. "No one, not even Grandma, knew about the argument between the first Senator Jukes and Great Grandpa. Not until now that is."

"Have you spoken to Grandma about this?"

"No, I wanted to bring it up after the Reynolds' left this evening, but Grandma had dozed off. I didn't want to wake her."

"It does seem strange, doesn't it? It gives me such an eerie feeling. It's like Aunt Charlotte's come back from the dead."

Logan chuckled. "Am I going to have to tuck you in to bed too? Check the closet and under your bed?" he teased his sister.

She returned the smile and shivered playfully. "You might. The hairs on my neck stand up every time I glance at that photo and see Aunt Charlotte. What if . . . well, what if the family was murdered? What if the fire wasn't an accident like everyone has assumed all these years?"

His brows creased. "I don't know. It would be interesting to find out more."

Beth sighed. "Well, if anyone can find out what really happened, it would be you." She smiled affectionately at her older brother. "I'm going to bed. Grandma tends to wake earlier all the time. She's in terrible pain, so she doesn't sleep well."

He nodded. He worried about Adelaide, and he answered, "I don't tell you often enough how grateful I am to you. I couldn't do this alone. I wouldn't know where to start."

"You'd be a mess," she laughed, shaking her head. Logan shared her smile before she suddenly frowned. "Sometimes I'm so afraid. I wonder how long she has left. I can't stand the thought of losing her. We've been so close over the years."

"She's lived a good life. She misses Grandpa but I am going to miss her, more than I want to admit."

"I know. I hate watching her grow so weak. I hate seeing her in pain. Some days it's so hard." She inhaled deeply and her shoulders fell. "Well, good night."

Logan watched as Beth left the office and walked down the hall toward her room. He turned back toward the wide window and stared out toward the gentle swells. Perhaps he would take that swim after all. Maybe it would help clear his mind.

* * * * * * *

Kadie rolled out of the uncomfortable motel bed. She stretched her stiff muscles and yawned. Taking a deep breath, she brushed her mangled, wild hair out of her face before she glanced over at Maysha, who was still sleeping soundly. Maysha could always sleep anywhere, but Kadie had spent the night tossing and turning on the lumpy mattress, and more nightmares had returned. Images of a house in flames and Adelaide's haunted eyes came rushing back. She stood, trying to push the dream away.

She walked to the window and glanced at the new morning before she turned to check the bedside clock. It was early enough for a morning jog, and she knew her sister wouldn't be awake for a couple of hours. Determined, she tiptoed into the bathroom to tidy her hair and get dressed. She had promised herself that she would get back in shape, and a brisk jog down to the waterfront and along the beach sounded great.

She left a hastily scribbled note on the nightstand for Maysha then left the motel room and stepped out into the crisp, new morning. Walking for a few minutes, she warmed her muscles and then started a slow jog in the direction of the waterfront park. It didn't take her long to reach the narrow strip of beach, and she turned onto the sand eagerly. It took a moment to adjust her gait to the new ground beneath her, but soon she jogged briskly along the water's edge. She enjoyed the new sensation, and she dodged the gentle waves that rolled onto the sand.

She passed several people along the long stretch of beach, and when she passed an older couple, walking hand-in-hand, her thoughts centered on Adelaide and Charlotte. What had happened to Charlotte? Why had her body never been found? *Poor Adelaide,* Kadie mused as the vivid images from her dream rushed to the front of her thoughts. She suppressed a shiver as she recalled her nightmare.

Kadie's eyes broadened and her lips parted when she realized she stood among the burned ruins of the Clarke home. Rain poured through the broken roof, soaking the charred beams and pooling in depressions along the wood floor. The house groaned like an angry animal, and she whimpered quietly. Fear stole up her back, and she shuddered as the musty, acrid smell of decaying earth filled her nostrils.

Suddenly, the ruin vanished and she found herself standing outside, surrounded by pinion pines and giant sandstone boulders. The wind burst through the trees and she turned, confused. Her eyes darted across the hills, and she was surprised to see Charlotte's house below, standing as it must have once looked. The home had a small yard, surrounded by a white picket fence. Snow blanketed the ground and covered the garden. Dead, brittle cornstalks bent against the breeze.

Her brow furrowed and she let out a startled gasp when she realized the roof was in flames. Fire licked at the wooden siding and burst through the glass windows. The sound of the splintering glass filled the night. Black smoke billowed high into the air, blocking the full moon from sight. The blaze lit up the sky. Light from the flames cast eerie shadows across the snow-covered hills, and Kadie tore her eyes from the house when she heard the unmistakable sound of her name carried on the wind.

The trees surrounding her moaned against the breeze. She glanced around her frantically and cried out when she realized Charlotte stood above her, only scant feet away. Her face was pale and horror-stricken. The flames reflected in the young girl's black eyes. Her white nightdress, smudged with mud and soot, billowed in the wind. Her long, black hair flowed about her gaunt shoulders and whipped across her face. Kadie's breath froze in her lungs and fear gripped her throat when Charlotte suddenly turned to face her. Their eyes locked just as Charlotte screamed Kadie's name, her voice shrill and terrifying.

Kadie had jerked awake, cold and shivering, with the sound of Charlotte's frightened shriek still ringing in her ears. She'd lain awake for another hour before she'd finally fallen into an exhausted slumber. She suppressed a shudder as she jogged around a large piece of driftwood. She had to focus on her run. She felt like a child, dreaming up ghosts and waking from nightmares in the middle of the night. *What is happening to me?* She groaned. Why was she allowing herself to get caught up in childish fantasies?

The sun shimmered against the soft waves, and she forced her thoughts away from Charlotte and the strange dream. She saw a large cliff face, looming before her. The rocky ledge jutted into the water and the surf sent mist high into the air as large waves broke against the craggy surface. The scene was beautiful and she longed to be closer, to feel the mist on her face. She passed another runner and waved before she forced her legs to pick up the pace.

Suddenly a hand grabbed her shoulder from behind. Startled, her eyes opened wide and she screamed. Her feet twisted in the soft sand, and she lurched forward. Her arms flayed desperately as she tried to regain her balance before she slammed against the ground. Several small pebbles and broken shells hidden in the sand dug into the palms, and she yelped before she spun around to face her pursuer.

CHAPTER *Seven*

"Kadence!" Logan hovered above her. A startled, worried frown marred his rugged features. "Kadie, I'm so sorry." He breathed. "Are you all right?"

Kadie's thin shoulders slumped with relief, and she let herself fall back in the sand. She gulped in a lungful of air before she spoke. "You scared me to death."

He moved next to her, bending over with his hands resting on his knees, and caught his breath. His dark face was covered in sweat and splotched from exertion. "I didn't mean to scare you. Are you hurt?" he asked as he knelt down in front of her.

She smelled the scent of his aftershave, and her already pounding heart skipped a beat. He reached over and grasped her hand in his. He brushed the sand and pebbles away to examine the few minor scrapes along her palm. His finger ran across the abrasions and their eyes met.

"I'm sorry," he murmured, and she held her breath when he suddenly leaned over to place a kiss against her open palm. She caught her breath and willed her heart to slow its quick rhythm.

He stood straight and assisted her to her feet. She stumbled slightly before she pulled her hand from his firm grasp and brushed the sand from her shorts and bare legs.

He watched her with a slight smile then spoke, "Wow, you can run! I spent the last ten minutes trying catch up to you."

Kadie laughed sheepishly. "I didn't hear anyone. I'm sorry. I didn't mean to get so bent out of shape. My thoughts were . . . wandering."

Logan grinned. "I called your name, but you didn't hear me. By the time I caught up to you, I was too out of breath to do anything but grab you. I didn't think I'd scare you so bad."

He laughed, and Kadie smiled. She liked the sound of his rich laughter. She took a deep breath. "What are you doing here?"

Logan turned and walked back toward the way they had just come. Kadie followed.

"I run this stretch of beach every morning. I just don't come this far." He laughed. "I saw you from a ways back. I was surprised to see you, so I thought I'd catch up. I thought we could run together." He exhaled. "But I didn't know you were a sprinter."

She laughed, shaking her head. "I wasn't paying any attention. I'm afraid to say I was thinking about Charlotte and Adelaide."

His smile faded. "You too, huh?" She watched at him curiously, but he said instead, "Where's your sister?"

"Back at the motel, probably still asleep," Kadie replied.

He nodded, and his heart-stopping smile returned. "Why don't we run back together? I'll take you up to the house so we can get those scratches taken care of, and there are a few things I'd like to discuss with you, if you don't mind."

Her eyebrows rose. What did he want to talk with her about? He glanced at her expectantly, and Kadie was quick to reply, "My hands are fine, honestly. I'm not exactly the most graceful person in the world, remember? I fell through a floor. But I'd love to talk. What about, exactly?"

He began a slow jog and Kadie kept pace. "Why don't we call the motel when we get back to my car? And Maysha can bring your vehicle around to the house whenever she feels up to it. Adelaide will be up early and I know she's anxious to see you again. She was very despondent after you two left yesterday. It was a nice visit for her. I don't know what sort of plans you and your sister had for today, but it won't take long. You don't mind?"

"We were going sight-seeing today, but I'd love to come back and visit with Adelaide."

"Great, then later we can talk about a few things," he panted as he picked up his pace.

Kadie matched her stride to his and they jogged down the narrow strip of beach in comfortable silence. She was anxious to discover what it was Logan wanted to talk with her about. She imagined it had something to do with Adelaide and Charlotte. It didn't take them long to reach Logan's silver BMW, and he held the door for her as she slid into the luxurious interior.

She used his cell phone to call Maysha. She knew her sister wasn't happy about their change of plans, and Kadie listened with a frown while Maysha blatantly voiced her opinion concerning "this ghost business" before she finally agreed to bring their car around. When Kadie shut the phone, Logan smiled perceptively.

"I'm afraid I've disturbed your plans."

She shook her head and stared out at the thick forest bordering the narrow lane leading to Logan's home. "No, not really, besides we still have a few days before we have to head back," she answered.

"Did the two of you have any definite plans for the day?"

She glanced at him, studying his sharp profile for a moment before she smiled. "No. We had thought about driving into Seattle, but . . . ." She shrugged. "We'll still have time to see the piers before we leave."

His mouth twisted. "Seattle is a good place to visit. Would you mind a personal tour? If you would like, I'd be happy to take you and Maysha today. We can take the ferry. I need to stop by my office for a moment, and . . . well, I'd like to see someone while we're in town. That's part of the reason I wanted to speak with you."

Kadie waited as Logan parked the BMW in front of the large house. She was anxious for him to continue, but they were distracted when Zaza burst from the house and ran down the front steps. Logan glanced at Kadie.

"I'll explain later," he murmured as he stepped from the car.

Kadie watched with a smile as Zaza launched herself into Logan's arms, and he caught her up, swinging her high into the air. Zaza's dark hair hung in wet masses down her back, and her cheeks were tinged pink. She grinned down at Logan and laughed.

"How's my mermaid this morning?" Logan asked.

"Hi, Daddy! Aunt Beth and I swam so much further today, and we saw the baby seals again," she crowed delightedly. She turned to face Kadie with a wide, toothless grin. "Good morning! Do you want to come and see my baby seals?" She laughed.

Logan set her down on her feet, and the little girl ran to grab hold of Kadie's hand. Kadie laughed and hugged her tight. "Hi, Zaza! I'd love to," she replied and glanced at Logan questioningly.

"Maybe later, princess. Kadie and I are going to visit Grandma this morning."

Zaza frowned and turned her face toward the ground. Her shoulders slumped, and Kadie squeezed the little girl's hand, smiling.

Once in the house, Beth greeted Kadie with a wide smile. "Well good morning!" She looked surprised, and she glanced between Logan and Kadie with a curious expression.

"Look who I ran into this morning—literally. We met each other running on the beach," he hastily explained.

"Where's Maysha?" Beth questioned.

"She'll be coming around soon," Logan answered, and then asked, "Is Grandma awake?"

Beth nodded and her eyes shot toward Kadie. "I'm glad you're here. Grandma was asking about Kadie. She wanted to speak with her again." She turned her gaze back to Logan and went on, "I was going to call you and ask you to phone her. Adelaide was determined. So this works out really well."

Logan's brow rose, surprised. "We'll go right up. Zaza, go and eat your breakfast. Kadie and I will be down soon." He tapped the little girl's nose playfully and she giggled.

"See ya," she called as she skipped into the kitchen.

Kadie's anxiety increased when they neared Adelaide's bedroom, and she followed Logan silently. She was excited to see Adelaide again, yet she felt nervous, almost on edge. She followed Logan into the small bedroom and caught sight of Adelaide sitting up in bed, bent over the small journal. Her long hair hung in a thick braid down her shoulder, and she wore a flowered-print nightdress. She didn't glance up as Logan approached the bed, and he reached his hand toward her.

Suddenly, Adelaide's head shot up and she glanced past Logan. She looked directly into Kadie's eyes. Kadie paused and the old woman smiled.

"You've come," she whispered and shut Charlotte's journal.

She placed the journal on the night stand, and Kadie caught sight of the old photograph propped against the bedside lamp. A shiver ran down the length of her spine as she glanced at Charlotte's smiling face. The sound of the young girl's voice screaming in the wind echoed in her mind, and she suppressed a shudder. Logan watched her expectantly, and she pulled her thoughts away from her morbid musing and approached Adelaide with a smile.

"Good morning," she greeted Adelaide when the older woman reached for Kadie's hand.

Immediately, Kadie felt a sense of kinship when she grasped the older woman's hand. All her fears over Charlotte seemed to dissipate as she stared into Adelaide's kind, vibrant eyes. Kadie leaned down and placed a soft kiss on her wrinkled cheek.

Adelaide patted her hand tenderly as she spoke. "I'm glad you've returned. She told me you would."

"Oh, yes. Beth said you wanted to see me again." She smiled. Adelaide's eyes narrowed and she looked momentarily confused.

"Beth?" Kadie glanced at Logan and was about to reply when Adelaide shook her head. "No, not Beth—Charlotte," she replied.

Kadie's lips parted and her eyes shot to Logan's. His brows creased, and he placed a hand against Adelaide's frail shoulder.

"Grandma," he began, "you must mean Beth. Charlotte—"

Adelaide shook her head, cutting him off, and she shot him a stern look. "Logan, I am not delusional. Don't treat me as if I am. In fact, I'm feeling very sure of my sanity this morning." She smiled again, and her eyes met Kadie's once more. "I saw her last night. She stood just where Kadence is standing," Adelaide whispered.

A shiver ripped up Kadie's spine, and she inhaled deeply as the stark images from her dream rushed to the surface. Adelaide went on, "My sister did not die in that fire. I am certain of that now. She's out there still . . . somewhere in those hills, beyond the house." She faced Logan while she finished. "I need to know what happened to my family and my sister."

Kadie watched him closely. The hairs on her arms stood up as she suppressed a shiver. Logan's mouth twisted, and he shook his head. "Grandma, I don't think . . . ." He paused and ran a hand through his thick hair.

Adelaide's watery eyes narrowed. "Logan, she's speaking to me. I need your help," she whispered. Her eyes found Kadie's, and Adelaide's cold fingers tightened against her hand. "You know. *You know.* She came to you too. This is no accident. You are here for a reason. There is a purpose for everything in this life. There are no accidents."

Kadie inhaled and tears stung the back of her eyes. "I . . . ," She began then she swallowed hard.

Her words caught in her throat. Emotion gripped her chest, and she felt as if she would sob. Charlotte's presence in the room was so tangible Kadie feared that if she turned around, the same image from her dream would suddenly materialize. She nodded weakly and then stole a glance at Logan.

His gaze met hers warily and he frowned. "Grandma, you're tired. Perhaps you should rest," he suggested.

Adelaide's grip on Kadie's hand loosened and the older woman gave Kadie one more pleading glance before she let her weak frame fall back against the bed. Adelaide sighed. Her eyelids closed slowly, and tears filled the deep wrinkles in the corner of her eyes.

"I can feel her. She's so close. So *very* close," she whispered. "You can feel her, Kadence. I know you can."

"Yes, I can," Kadie replied. Her voice was nearly inaudible.

Adelaide's eyes opened once more. Weakly, she reached for Logan. He grabbed his grandmother's hand. Bringing it to his lips, he kissed it gently. "Please, Logan," she implored, "if anyone can find out what happened to Charlotte, you can."

Logan's expression faltered, and Kadie read the wary emotions in his eyes. He exhaled and gazed toward Adelaide with a reluctant smile. "Alright, Grandma, I'll do what I can. Please, try to get some rest."

A weak smile touched the older woman's thin lips, and her eyes closed again. Her chest rose, and Kadie watched while Adelaide fell into a swift, peaceful slumber. She felt Logan's dark eyes on her, and she reluctantly turned to meet his questioning gaze. She remained silent as he studied her for a moment. Her heart pounded against her chest. Her eyes left his, and her gaze unwillingly fell on the photograph.

She shuddered. She *could* feel Charlotte, as crazy as it seemed.

Adelaide's sister's presence was as real as she. She tore her eyes from the black-and-white photo and studied Adelaide's face, relaxed in sleep. Kadie's heart faltered, and she touched the elderly woman's hand. Once again that strange, almost unearthly bond assailed her, tying her to Adelaide. Kadie couldn't help wonder if that strange, unexplainable bond between her and Adelaide wasn't Charlotte's influence as well.

Logan suddenly cleared his throat, and Kadie tore her eyes from Adelaide. She met his gaze hesitantly. With a frown, he stepped toward her and grasped her elbow. His brow furrowed. "She'll sleep like that for hours. We need to talk," he spoke.

She remained silent, and her heart beat an unfamiliar pattern as Logan led her down the hall and into his spacious office. He shut the door and motioned to a chair. "Have a seat."

She eyed him warily when he stepped around his desk and sat in his expensive swivel chair. He grasped a folder from off a shelf and turned toward the desk. She sat silent and watched as he flipped the folder open and read the first page. Nervous, she took a moment to glance around the room. The room's furnishings added a very masculine feel to the room, and she studied a seascape painting against the far wall as Logan's eyes fell on her once again.

She felt his penetrating gaze and cautiously, she peeled her eyes away from the painting to meet his.

"Could you . . ." He paused and licked his lips. "Can you explain what Adelaide was talking about, please?"

Kadie's hands shook, and she took a deep breath. She was feeling shaken and disoriented. She wondered if she wasn't going a little insane. "I . . . I don't know, Logan. Ever since I've found that journal . . . I can't explain the way I feel," she replied.

"Try. Please?" he implored, and Kadie's eyes jumped to his.

Her brow furrowed, and she regarded him hesitantly. She read no mockery or anger in his expression, just curiosity. Could she explain the way she felt to Logan when she really didn't understand it herself? She studied his expression for a moment longer. Certain she read no contempt or distrust in his eyes, she tried to explain. "I dreamed about her last night. For the past couple of nights, for that matter. I see the house as it must have once looked. I see their home as it looks now. I've seen . . . her. I hear her voice in my head.

"Ever since I found that coffee can and I read her journal, I can't get her out of my head . . . out of my thoughts. After I read her journal, I knew I had to find Adelaide. I just felt like I *had* to find her. Like some invisible string was suddenly drawing me here. It feels like . . . as if Charlotte's been guiding me here all along. Maysha thinks I'm crazy. I know it sounds insane, but it's as if I were meant to find that journal and then find you . . . Adelaide, I mean. I know it sounds crazy, but I felt *something* inside that house—a presence. I heard a whisper. I've never believed in ghosts or spirits coming back to haunt, but this . . . it's crazy—unbelievable," she finished, her voice barely above a whisper. *Logan thinks I'm insane.* She didn't dare look up.

"No, not crazy," he answered slowly, "incredulous maybe, but not crazy." Relieved, Kadie's eyes shot to his, and he ran a hand along his square jaw line.

"I don't put a lot of stock in ghosts and haunting spirits myself, but I've lived with Adelaide for most of my life, and I've never heard her talk like this. She's always been very open about Aunt Charlotte, the fire, and her family. But it's never been like this. I don't believe she's delusional, but I can't explain what is happening." He shrugged.

She studied his expression. "So you believe me?"

His frown deepened, but he nodded. Kadie felt stunned. She'd expected him to laugh in her face or worse, toss her out on her backside. Robert would have laughed and called her a fool, and the thought of Robert's condescending voice made her angry.

Logan sat back in his chair and stared at the files on his desk, his expression contemplative. "Kadie," he began. His brow furrowed. "The reason I wanted to speak with you today sounds a bit incredulous as well."

She leaned in closer. "What is it?"

"Last night I was curious. I spent the better part of the night researching the Jukes family—their history, the politics, and well—I discovered Adam Jukes' most recent address. He's quite old, obviously only a few years younger than Adelaide. I'm not certain of his state of health, but he lives with his youngest son, Kenny Jukes.

"Kenny Jukes was elected to the House of Representatives, but he's currently retried. His children live in Washington as well. His daughter married the son a wealthy business owner. His oldest son, Jackson, and his youngest son, Bradley, are both members of the House committee. The Jukes family seems to be a very prominent political family. I don't know what our chances are, but I'd like to speak with Adam Jukes. He was at Adelaide's parent's home the night of the fire. It would be interesting to know his take on the situation. Perhaps he remembers details of that night and can help shed some light on what might have happened. For all we know, it was a horrifying accident."

"Do you really believe the fire was an accident?" Kadie asked.

"I've always believed it was. Aunt Charlotte's disappearance has always bothered Adelaide, but she's never doubted the fire was indeed an unfortunate accident. Grandpa Moss always believed that Charlotte's body was simply never recovered from the rubble. However, nobody has ever mentioned the former Senator's visit to the Clarke home that night. I doubt anyone ever knew of it. Certainly not Adelaide or Fred, and until now . . . well, I can't help but feel . . . and I may be off my rocker, but I have a feeling that the fire had *everything* to do with the Jukes' visit that night."

"And you're hoping that Adam Jukes will confess to what—arson? Murder?" Beth's voice suddenly cut into the conversation. Kadie jumped slightly, startled to see Beth standing behind her. She hadn't heard her come in. Logan's sister stepped into the office and sat on a chair next to Kadie. She smiled a weak greeting then continued, "I'm just not sure what you're expecting to find, Logan."

Logan sighed. "I don't either. This really is crazy, isn't it?"

Kadie watched Beth apprehensively, but remained silent.

"Yes, and I'm worried. Maybe the past should just stay put," Beth suggested. Logan exhaled loudly and pushed back from his desk. The silence in the office seemed almost ominous. After a long moment, Beth took a deep breath. "This means so much to her, doesn't it?" She glanced at Kadie. "You should have heard her earlier, talking about Aunt Charlotte. Personally, I'm scared to death. I wish that journal had never been found."

Kadie cringed. She hadn't ever thought about the possible negative consequences of returning Charlotte's journal. Beth's eyes swung to meet Kadie's, and she smiled apologetically.

"Oh, Kadie, I'm sorry! I . . . I didn't mean anything." The other woman reached over and grasped Kadie's hand.

"I really never thought . . . well, I never thought that it would upset her so badly," Kadie apologized.

"No," Beth soothed. "It wasn't anyone's fault. She couldn't have been happier when we handed her Aunt Charlotte's things. And if the fire—"

"We don't know anything yet," Logan cut in. "For all we know the fire was an accident. I just thought that I'd like to find out more, if in fact there is anything more to find. I doubt we'll learn anything further than what we already know." He sighed. "But this is very important to Grandma, and I'd like to do what I can."

Kadie remained silent while Beth contemplated Logan's words. She glanced toward Kadie then back to Logan. "Just be careful, please," she whispered. "I have a terrible feeling about this."

Logan rubbed a finger across his chin absently then asked, "So, what do you think? Would you come along with me to speak with Senator Jukes? It shouldn't take too long, and afterwards I will be more than happy to show you and Maysha around the city. I know of a fantastic café along the pier. We can eat lunch and be back here before nightfall."

Surprised, Kadie smiled. She was pleased Logan wanted her to accompany him to visit Senator Jukes. She was inexplicably happy for the chance to spend a day with him.

"Yes," she answered, "I'd love to go along. Maysha will be thrilled to visit Seattle."

A grin replaced Logan's dour expression. "Great. We'll leave as soon as Maysha gets here."

Kadie's smile faltered when she caught sight of Beth's worried face. She squeezed the woman's hand, and Beth repeated, "Please, just be careful."

CHAPTER *Eight*

"Okay, I could seriously be very happy living here," Maysha commented while she and Kadie viewed Seattle's main business district from the comfort of Logan's vehicle.

Logan grinned and glanced in the rearview mirror. "There are some pretty amazing universities around here too."

Maysha nodded thoughtfully. "Really?"

Kadie chuckled. "Don't even think about it, Maysha. You can't leave me in Utah all alone."

"Alone?" Her sister snorted. "After December you'll have your hands full with Robert and his mom, and how often do you think 'Dear Robert' and 'Mother' are going to let me visit?" She laughed. "She's getting *married*," Maysha directed at Logan.

Embarrassed, Kadie felt a deep blush creep her neck. She caught sight of Logan's surprised expression, and she smiled sheepishly.

"Married?" He grinned. "I didn't realize you were engaged, Kadie."

"Umm . . . Robert is a dentist," she stammered. Logan's eyebrows rose. "And we're getting married in December," she finished lamely. Kadie cringed. Why did it matter if Logan knew if she were engaged?

"Really?" His eyes fell on her bare finger and she shrugged.

"I don't have the ring yet. Robert . . . it's an old family heirloom. It needed to be resized. It was too small," she hastened to explain.

Maysha laughed and jumped in. "That's because all the women in dear Robert's family have all been petite, nagging old biddies. You've been engaged for almost a year, and you don't have the ring yet because good ole' Rob's mother refused to give it back."

Kadie's teeth ground together and her blush deepened. "Maysha!"

Logan chuckled, and Kadie rushed to explain. "Maysha and Robert don't get along well."

"Awww . . . I see." He winked at Maysha.

"Well, personally, I'll never understand what you see in him. Why *are* you still marrying him?"

"Maysha!" Kadie retorted. "Would you please stop? We can talk about this later."

Her sister laughed, unrepentant. "Oh, come on. I know you've been asking yourself the same thing," she pressed, then addressed Logan. "I've been trying to talk her out of this engagement for months now. Maybe you can help."

Kadie choked then coughed. Her cheeks flamed red, and she glared at her sister, stunned.

Logan caught Kadie's eye briefly. "Maybe," he answered. A slow smile spread across his face, and he chuckled.

Her cheeks warmed, and her heart skipped a beat. Catching sight of Maysha's smug face, Kadie scowled. *I'll strangle her in her sleep*, she vowed silently. She turned and stared out the window, feeling mortified while she did her best to focus her thoughts on Seattle's Waterfront district. When she saw a sign indicating Pike Place Market, she pointed toward it.

"I've heard of Pike Place," she spoke, hoping to change the subject.

Her voice sounded breathless and strained. Maysha eyed her with a mocking smile, and Kadie glared at her sister.

"It's a great little spot for shopping. We could take a few hours later this afternoon to visit the market," Logan responded.

"Yes! Please!" Maysha groaned from the back seat. Then she added, "In fact, I have an even better idea! Why don't you drop me off here before you two resume your ghost hunt? I have absolutely no desire to meet this man or talk about ghosts. Besides, I need double the time to shop—just ask Kadie." Her voice rose.

Logan's mouth twisted in thought and he pulled the car off to the side of the busy street. He parked and turned to face Kadie. "What do you think?"

"That would be fine, I guess," she responded.

He turned toward Maysha. "We'll call when we're finished with Senator Jukes. We can meet up for lunch at a café near the market. It's a little place right below the fish mart."

"Great." Maysha slid out of the backseat. "See ya!" she called.

Kadie waved as Logan pulled the car back onto the busy road, and the silence in the car deepened.

"I . . . ," she began, "I'm sorry about that. Maysha is . . . well, she's—"

Logan laughed, cutting her off. "She's a riot! Besides, she's a little sister, right? I have one myself." Kadie laughed, relieved. "I'm glad you understand. And Beth is great. You two seem very close."

He shrugged and nodded. "We weren't always this close, especially after our parent's death. She took it pretty hard. We all did, but over the years, I guess you could say we learned to depend on each other. I don't know where I'd be without her, especially since my divorce. Zaza and I would have been in real trouble without Beth around."

She glanced at Logan. She had wondered more than once about Zaza's mother. She wanted to broach the subject, but she said instead, "I'm sorry about your parents. What happened?"

"It was a car accident. They were there, and then suddenly, they were gone. I was sixteen. Grandma and Grandpa raised the three of us. It couldn't have been easy either—raising three orphaned teenagers."

"Three of you?"

"Beth, Jace, and I. Beth was twelve, Jace was fifteen and like I said, I was sixteen, almost seventeen. Jace is an accountant in New York, and Beth, well . . . Beth has put her whole life on hold. First she helped Grandma take care of Grandpa, and now she's taking care of the rest of us."

Kadie was thoughtful for a moment. The pain at losing her own parents still weighed on her mind.

"So," Logan's deep voice cut into Kadie's thoughts. "Why are you marrying Robert?"

Taken aback, Kadie stammered, "I . . . oh . . . well—" She paused, wondering how to answer. *Maysha*, she thought angrily.

Logan studied her distressed expression and chuckled. "Remind me to ask again later. We're here." He pointed ahead.

Surprised, she glanced out the window. She hadn't been paying any attention. They were traveling through an upscale neighborhood, and she whistled quietly when Logan parked next to the curb in front of a brick, colonial-style home. Remarkable picture rail moldings, double-hung windows, and a large sunroom defined the home. The lawn was immaculate and a cobbled walk led to an ornately carved, walnut door.

Kadie placed a hand against her fluttering stomach, and Logan winked before he stepped from the car. He stepped around the vehicle and held her door while she slid from the comfort of his car. They walked silently up the front walk. Logan rang the bell, and within moments the door swung open. An older, white-haired woman greeted them with a scowl.

"Can I help you?"

"Yes." Logan smiled, "I'm Logan Matthews, and this is Kadence Reynolds. We're hoping we can speak with former Senator Adam Jukes."

"Logan Matthews?" the older woman questioned stiffly. "Are you the lawyer who handled the state auditor's scandal?"

Kadie glanced at Logan. He nodded. "I am."

The woman's thin, penciled brows rose, and she stepped back. "I'm Lillian Jukes. Come on in. I'll see if my husband, Kenny, is available to speak with you."

Kadie remained silent while Lillian led them through the entry way and into a spacious living area. The floor was hardwood throughout the house, and the various decorations and paintings that adorned the walls reeked of wealth.

"Please, have a seat." Lillian Jukes directed them to an expensive leather sofa before she promptly left the room. Kadie caught Logan's eye momentarily, and she sat on the cushy couch with a nervous sigh. A large grandfather clock chimed from a distant room, and she glanced around curiously. An elaborate grand piano took up the far end of the spacious room. Exotic plants grew in huge, ornamental pots, and the room smelled of sandalwood and leather.

Soon heavy footfalls echoed down the hall and Kadie watched with wide eyes when a large man stepped into the room. She guessed he was easily in his mid-sixties. His clothing looked stylish and immaculate. His white hair and goatee were trimmed neatly, and he looked lean and muscular for his age.

Logan stood and greeted the man, "Mr. Jukes."

"Logan Matthews, I was hoping you and I would get a chance to meet, and here you are! What do I owe the pleasure of your visit?"

"It's good to meet you, sir. I've heard great things about you."

"Yes, and I've heard fantastic things about you as well. The way you handled Farrington's case was pure genius. Have you ever considered running for DA?"

Logan chuckled, and Kadie eyed him wonderingly. Beth had told her and Maysha that Logan was a lawyer, but she hadn't realized just how successful he was.

"I haven't considered that course quite yet," Logan replied modestly.

"Well, if you ever do, you can count on my support," Kenny Jukes bellowed and slapped him on the shoulder.

"I appreciate that, Mr. Jukes."

"Oh, please, call me Kenny. And it seems as if I've forgotten all my manners." Kenny Jukes glanced toward Kadie. He raised his hand to grasp hers. "And who is this beautiful lady? Mrs. Matthews, I presume?" He grinned.

Kadie blushed. "No! Oh, no. I'm Kadence Reynolds, a friend. I'm pleased to meet you, Mr. Jukes."

"I see—well, have a seat." Kenny Jukes indicated the sofa, and she sat next to Logan.

She caught Logan's teasing smile and, feeling slightly flustered, she scowled.

"Now, what do I owe the pleasure?" Kenny asked as he sat opposite them in a large, leather recliner.

"Well," Logan began, "we're actually here on some old family business. We came to speak with Senator Adam Jukes. It seems our families knew one another. They originated in the same town."

"Is that so?" Kenny's head lifted, and his eyes seemed to darken.

Kadie wondered if perhaps she had just imagined the change, and she studied Kenny as he went on.

"Small world, isn't it? Tell me, how did they know one another?"

"It seems my grandmother knew Adam Jukes when they were children. They lived in a little town called Eureka—in Utah."

"Ah—yes, the Jukes clan does originate in Utah. My father was born and raised in Eureka. You say your grandmother knew the Jukes family?"

Logan nodded. "Yes, Adelaide Clarke. She was only a few years older than Adam."

"Well, how interesting," Kenny replied, and Kadie was certain she could detect a change in his countenance. His body stiffened, and he regarded Logan suspiciously. She wondered if Logan had noticed the change in Kenny Jukes, but he only nodded and smiled congenially. He gave no indication he'd noticed Kenny Jukes' sudden change.

"Well, Dad is in his study. He and I were catching a few reruns of the Seahawks' last season. Why don't you two come on back?"

Kenny stood and Logan reached for Kadie's hand, helping her from the couch. They followed Kenny through the immaculate house. They turned down a long hallway, and she eyed the collection of photos covering the walls. Some were black-and-white and many were in color, and she noticed most of the photos were taken in caves or near caverns.

A number of large prints depicted the intricate, colorful interior of several caverns. More than a few black-and-white photos centered on a man, similar in looks and size to Kenny Jukes, dressed in spelunking gear, standing by the mouth of different caves. Kadie could only assume he was the former Senator. *I guess he likes spelunking,* she noted.

"Here we are," Kenny spoke when they neared a darkened room.

Kadie held her breath, and her stomach turned when they entered the room. Logan's hand tightened against hers, and she glanced up at him before he turned his attention to a frail man, sitting in a wheelchair. Adam Jukes sat in front of several flat plasma screens, and a football game played across the screens. The old man glanced at Logan and Kadie with curious, alert eyes.

"We have visitors, Dad." Kenny reached for a remote and switched off the televisions.

"Is that so?" Adam turned in his chair to greet Logan with a handshake. His eyes were friendly. "And what do we owe the pleasure of having Attorney Logan Matthews visit?

"Senator, it's nice to meet you," Logan replied.

"Nice work on your latest case, counselor. I watched you very closely through that ordeal. You handled it superbly."

"Thank you, I appreciate that." Logan nodded respectfully.

"It seems that our families have an old connection," Kenny cut in.

"Ah—how so?" Adam's countenance brightened.

"Well, both of our families were from Eureka, Utah," Logan began.

Kadie wasn't surprised when Adam's smile faltered and his thin frame tensed. A knowing glance passed between father and son as Logan went on.

"My grandmother is Adelaide Clarke," Logan told them.

Immediate recognition showed plainly on Adam Jukes' face, and Kadie heard the rush of air as he breathed deep through his nostrils.

"It seems as though our families knew one another," Logan finished.

"Yes—the name does sound vaguely familiar. However, my family moved away from Eureka when I was a young man. My father was elected to the Utah State Senate, and we moved directly to Salt Lake City."

"Well, it may have been that you were closer to her brother Alvin's age?" Logan added.

Adam Jukes remained silent for a moment, and his watery eyes lowered toward the ground. He nodded slowly. "Yes . . . yes, I do recall Al Clarke. How is good ole' Al getting on in years?" he asked, not quite meeting Logan's eyes.

"He died in a fire, if you recall? The whole family in fact," Logan responded, watching him.

The old man's face paled, and his wrinkled, frail hands shook slightly. "Fire?" he questioned.

Kadie could detect a definite false note in his voice. Kenny tensed, and he watched his father apprehensively.

"Yes, a fire. It was a terrible tragedy. All but Adelaide died that night, and it appears there is quite a mystery." Logan paused and eyed the Jukes men. "You see every body was recovered—everyone's body but Charlotte Clarke's. If you recall, Charlotte was Adelaide's twin sister."

Adam's mouth trembled, and he licked his dry lips nervously. "I don't recall. What a terrible thing. My family must have left town previously."

Logan smiled calmly. "Not quite." He pulled the journal from his back pocket. "You see, all these years, the cause of the fire has always been a mystery. No one really knows what happened that night. Amazingly enough, Ms. Reynolds was exploring the old foundation of the Clarke home, and she happened to find a can, hidden within the foundation of the old home. The can contained this journal." He held the small book higher so the Jukes men could clearly see. "It belonged to Charlotte," he finished.

Adam's mouth fell open and his eyes watered as he stared at the journal in Logan's hand. Fear seemed carved in every line of his face, and his breath came in shallow spurts.

"Charlotte's last entry mentions you and your father's visit to the Clarke home the night of the fire. It seems that your father, the late Senator Jukes, and Adelaide's father, had quite an argument that night," Logan stated.

Kenny watched his father closely, and his eyes narrowed before he turned to face Logan. "What exactly are you trying to say, Mr. Matthews?"

Adam stared hard at the floor and his mouth trembled visibly.

"Nothing at all. I'm simply hoping since you and your father, Senator, were there in the home the night of the fire, perhaps you could help shed some light on what may have happened," Logan directed at Adam.

Adam's eyes rose slowly, and anger smoldered deep in their vibrant depths. "No!" he spoke. "I'm afraid I don't recall that night. My father visited many people who lived in town. However, Charlotte Clarke was a menace. A troublemaker! People in town never doubted she started that fire and ran away."

"So you do recall the night of the fire?"

"Yes, I suppose I do, but an old man's memory is often full of holes. I'm tired, as you can see." Adam turned to his son. "Wheel me to my room."

Kenny placed his hands on Adam's wheelchair. Kenny's face was balmy and pale, and he glared at both Logan and Kadie. "Please see yourself out," he spoke curtly and wheeled Senator Jukes past without another glance.

"Perhaps we'll be in touch," Logan called.

Kenny paused and turned. "Please don't! Leave my house at once!"

The bright afternoon sun hurt Kadie's eyes as they left the dim interior of the Jukes' home and stepped outside. She took a deep, shaky breath and glanced at Logan. He smiled but remained silent as he opened her door. She slid into the interior of his BMW and watched as he hurried around to the driver's side and jumped behind the steering wheel. She turned and studied the house. A blind lifted in the far window, and she shivered, knowing they were being watched.

Logan started the car and pulled away from the curb. She felt anxious to know what he was thinking, but thought it best to remain silent until he was ready to speak. She clamped her trembling hands tightly in her lap. The Jukes men had certainly acted guilty. What had happened that night? Was Adam covering for his father, the late Senator Jukes? Kadie wondered if they had stumbled on a nearly century-old murder case. Her mind filled with questions and she looked to Logan. He appeared deep in thought.

They drove silently through the congested streets of Seattle and back toward the piers. She watched the city go by, and she was startled when Logan finally spoke.

"Well, what did you think?" he asked.

"Honestly?" she questioned with a self-conscious laugh.

"Honestly. I'd like to know what you're thinking."

Kadie shrugged. "Well, I don't think either senator will help you win an election now.

Logan chuckled. "I guess not."

"And I think those men are hiding something," she finished. "What do you think?"

"The same. It doesn't take an expert to know they were lying, and I believe they are hiding something. I have a feeling the esteemed Jukes family just may have a deep, dark secret."

"Do you think the fire was deliberately set?" Kadie questioned.

"Yes, and I think Senator Jukes knows exactly who is responsible. I also believe Charlotte Clarke was not in that house, and maybe it's the lawyer in me, but I think the Senator knows exactly what happened to Aunt Charlotte," Logan finished.

Charlotte's voice sounded in Kadie's head again, and she rubbed her arms, trying to suppress a shudder. "What do we do?"

Logan's brows furrowed. "I honestly hadn't thought this far ahead. We have no evidence—nothing to tie the Jukes' family to the fire. Well, nothing except a seventy-four year old journal. And it doesn't prove anything but the fact that the Jukes family had contact with the victims on the night in question."

She suppressed a smile. He sounded precisely like a lawyer. "So, besides an outright confession, we have nothing to go on?"

His lips twisted thoughtfully before he spoke. "You say the foundation of the home is still intact.

Kadie shivered as she recalled the haunted feeling she had standing within the burned remains.

"Part of the kitchen is still discernible, and some of the walls are still standing," she responded. "You can still smell the charred wood," she finished with a whisper. Charlotte's presence suddenly felt very strong. She wondered if Logan could feel it too. "What do you think happened to her?" she asked, her voice trembling.

"There's only one way to find out. Her body was never found," Logan replied, "and after seventy-five years, the chance of finding Aunt Charlotte's body is slim-to-none, but there may be other clues—evidence that was overlooked all those years ago. The snow on the ground during that time of year would have made the search for Charlotte's body, if she did in fact leave the house, very difficult as well."

He pulled the car alongside the curb and Kadie noticed they were once again on Alaskan Way, near Pike Place Market. He turned off the ignition and faced her.

"I think I'd like to take a trip out to Utah. I want to have a look around the old house," he told her.

She felt a sudden thrill, but chided herself. She had no place in all of this.

"It's an idea anyway," he added, then suggested, "Why don't we call Maysha and meet up for lunch?"

CHAPTER *Nine*

After a quick lunch at the café, they spent a few more hours shopping and exploring Seattle. Maysha wasted no time spending the majority of her hard-earned savings in the little shops situated along Seattle's waterfront. The afternoon went by quickly, and by the time Logan pulled the vehicle into his circular driveway, Kadie felt exhausted. She and Maysha had agreed to visit with Adelaide once more before returning to their motel.

"Boy, I'm beat," Maysha muttered as they stepped from his car.

Logan turned to face Kadie. "How many more days were you planning on staying in Washington?"

She shrugged. "Our plans aren't really in place. We're just sort of—"

"Winging it." Maysha finished.

Logan chuckled. "Well, how do you feel about spending a few more days ghost hunting?"

Immediately, Kadie's stomach filled with butterflies. "Yes!"

Maysha's shoulders slumped exaggeratedly, and Logan laughed outright. "Well, I was thinking . . . ," He looked to Maysha. "If you don't mind that is . . . ." He grinned and faced Kadie once again. "I want to beg a ride back to Salt Lake. I'm going to rent a jeep and travel on to Eureka. You can show me the old foundation, and we could start our search at the house. We'll see what we find and then go from there. What do you think?"

Kadie's stomach clenched at his use of pronouns, and she hoped Maysha would, for once, keep her mouth shut about Robert. *I seriously need to take some time to reconsider the reasons I'm still engaged to him*, she thought. She knew she shouldn't be so eager to spend more time with Logan, but the thought of spending more time in his company left her feeling giddy.

"Stay for dinner—please. I know Beth would love the chance to visit with you again," Logan added.

She glanced at her sister, pleading.

Maysha shrugged. "Beats pizza."

Kadie laughed but gave her sister a probing look. She wondered why Maysha was suddenly being so agreeable. It wasn't like her, and she observed Maysha carefully as they followed Logan up the stairs and into the house.

Maysha's lips curved into a smile, and she whispered, "What? Don't you *want* to stay for dinner?"

Kadie rolled her eyes, and Maysha giggled.

"You came back!" Zaza suddenly burst into the hallway, and the little girl ran past Logan and into Kadie's arms.

Surprised, Kadie returned the little girl's tight embrace.

"Can we go see the baby seals now, pleeeeaaaase?" Zaza plead, smiling.

Logan laughed. Tugging on Zaza's ponytails gently, he responded, "Why don't we invite Kadie and Maysha to dinner first, then we'll talk more about the baby seals, princess."

Zaza's eyes grew larger. "Can you please stay for dinner? Oh please, oh please?"

Logan and Kadie shared a smile.

"I'd love to stay for dinner," she replied.

Zaza hugged her tightly then latched onto Maysha, "You too, right?"

Her sister patted the little girl's back awkwardly. "Sure—whatever, kiddo," she mumbled just as Zaza caught sight of Maysha's shopping bags.

The little girl's eyes grew excited. "You went shopping! Can I see? Please, please?"

Maysha suppressed a scowl. "You like shopping?"

"Oh, yes, but Aunt Beth and Daddy don't take me," she pouted.

Maysha looked at Logan with shocked eyes. "That's just cruel and unusual punishment, Mr. Matthews. Come and see what I bought today, kid." A small smiled touched her lips.

Logan laughed and placed his hand on Kadie's shoulder when Maysha and Zaza disappeared into a sitting room off to the left of the kitchen. Surprised, Kadie caught his eye and he shrugged. "Two of a kind, huh?"

She returned his smile just as her cell phone rang. She jumped a little and pulled away from Logan to answer. Realizing it was Robert, she gasped. She had forgotten all about her fiancé.

"I . . . I should probably take this call." She turned to Logan. He considered her coolly.

He nodded, his smile disappearing. "You're welcome to use the office upstairs. It will afford you a bit more privacy."

"Thank you," she responded before she ascended the large staircase.

She reached Logan's office and stepped inside, shutting the door behind her. She glanced around. The desk was slightly disorganized. The files he'd been reading earlier in the day still lay strewn across the top, but the room was neat and smelled of Logan. She sighed. She was not looking forward to her conversation with Robert. She hit redial and waited patiently for him to answer.

"Kadie?" he answered, sounding petulant as usual.

"Hi, Robert. I forgot to call. I'm sorry," Kadie rushed to respond.

He remained silent for a long moment before he asked, "Where are you?"

Kadie bit down hard on her bottom lip, trying to keep her temper in check. "I'm at Adelaide's house with her family. We're getting ready to have dinner."

"I see."

"Do you?" Kadie asked.

"This ridiculous ghost hunt of yours has gone on long enough. You need to come home—now!" he demanded. "You have no idea how you've hurt Mother, taking off like you did, and now you're chasing some ridiculous notion." He paused for just a moment. "I've had it with this childishness."

Shocked, she took a deep breath. "What exactly do you mean?"

"I've tried calling several times today! I finally spoke with Maysha. You know, I used to consider you a fairly level-headed woman, but this is just plain crazy—not at all like you."

"Robert, you don't know the first thing about me. I don't believe you ever have," she responded. "Rob, you and I . . . ."

"*Robert*. It's *Robert*, Kadie! I hate being called Rob. You sound just like Maysha—heaven forbid!" he cut in sharply.

Kadie pinched the bridge of her nose and silently counted to ten before she responded, "*Robert*—I think it's time that you and I both face the facts. We're too different. This marriage would have never worked. I can't marry you. I'm sorry, but it's over. This should have happened months ago. I don't want to hurt you, but it's time."

"What do you mean? That's ridiculous. You can't possibly mean that," Robert replied.

She breathed slowly, and her shoulders relaxed. Without a doubt, she did not love Robert any longer, but she hated to hurt him. Tears stung the back of her eyes. "I'm sorry. I don't love you. Not anymore," she whispered. "I don't want to hurt you, but if we were both being honest, I think you would say the same. This . . . our marriage wouldn't have lasted," she added. "It's over."

"So you're saying that you're giving my ring back?" he asked incredulously.

Kadie sighed. "I don't exactly have a ring to give back."

"So, just like that, it's over? And what exactly do you expect me to tell Mother?"

Kadie's teeth ground together, and she groaned, "I don't know, Rob. Be creative. I'm sorry, I am, but goodbye."

She shut the cell phone without waiting for his reply. She took a deep, calming breath, and her hands trembled. She could scarcely believe she had just broken her engagement to Robert, but it had been a long time coming. She wished she'd had the courage to have done it sooner. She wondered what Maysha had told him, and she rubbed her brow wearily. Actually, she didn't care to know. Whatever her sister had said, it didn't matter. It was done. She knew her timing was rotten. It would have been more considerate to break their engagement face-to-face, but there was no sense in prolonging the inevitable, and she couldn't help but feel a terrible weight had been lifted.

Relaxing, she lifted her eyes to gaze out the wide window. Suddenly, her eyes met another's. Her lips parted and fear ripped up her spine as the image of a young woman in a white nightdress with long, dark hair stared back at her. A shrill scream tore from Kadie's throat and immediately the image vanished. Kadie stepped back, tripping over Logan's large desk chair. She hit the floor with a loud thump and she covered her head as the chair clattered to the floor beside her. Within moments, loud footsteps sounded outside the office, and Logan burst through the door.

"Kadie, what's wrong? Are you all right?" he asked, breathless.

His eyes grew large when he saw her sprawled on the floor, and he stepped into the office to help her to her feet. He righted the chair and eyed her with concern. Kadie stared at the darkened window. Her own reflection stared back. She raised a hand toward her throat and tore her eyes from the window. She hadn't imagined Charlotte's image, but the idea that she had just seen Charlotte was crazy . . . unbelievable.

"Kadie?" Logan looked confused, "What is it?"

She took a deep, shuddering breath. "Nothing . . . it's nothing. I'm sorry. I was just . . . startled. I thought I saw—"

Maysha suddenly burst into the office. "What's wrong?"

Kadie shook her head. "Nothing." She forced a chuckle. "It was just my imagination running wild. Something startled me. That's all."

Logan eyed her, his expression guarded. "Alright—everything else okay?" he questioned.

"Yes—I'm sorry. I'm fine, really."

Maysha frowned. "Geeze, Kadie! Scare us all to death, why don't you?"

She snorted then turned and stomped back down the stairs, leaving Kadie alone with Logan. Suddenly feeling very foolish, Kadie smiled sheepishly. His brow furrowed.

"Kadie—I . . . ," he paused, and she held her breath. *He thinks I'm crazy. Maybe I am crazy.* She caught her bottom lip between her teeth.

"I'm fine. Honestly," she tried to reassure him.

He exhaled. "Okay. Beth has dinner ready, whenever you are."

Her heart was still racing, but she peeked toward the window. She saw only her and Logan's reflection in the dark glass. She inhaled and nodded. She was eager to leave the office. "I'm ready."

* * * * * * *

Logan sat at the large dinner table, listening to the happy chatter and laughter that filled the vast kitchen. Kadie visited with Zaza, and Maysha and Beth gossiped happily about the latest entertainment news. He heard Kadie laugh and Zaza giggle. He watched Kadie out of the corner of his eye. He liked the way she laughed. She had a nice laugh that didn't grate on the nerves, and he enjoyed having her around. In fact, he enjoyed their new company far too much.

He liked seeing Beth making new friends. She didn't get out nearly enough, and she and Maysha had seemed to hit it off right from the start. He glanced at Kadie once again, and she caught his eye with a curious smile. He returned her smile before she turned her attention back to Zaza. Zaza had been immediately drawn to her, and he enjoyed watching his daughter interact with Kadie. He wondered about Kadie's fiancé. What sort of man was he?

Since his divorce, Logan hadn't really dated. He hadn't found anyone who held his interest for long, and too often the women he dated saw only dollar signs when they looked his way. He'd learned fast what lengths some women were willing to go to land a wealthy attorney. The thought made him cringe. Kadie, however, seemed different. She didn't have the edge that so many women he knew had. She was very intelligent, ambitious, and curious, but there was also a softness about her that shone in her countenance. He had to admit that finding out Kadence Reynolds was unavailable left him feeling rather depressed.

When she'd received the call earlier in the evening, it hadn't taken much to discern it was Robert on the phone. He wondered about their conversation. He felt curious. What had frightened Kadie so bad? She'd been as white as a ghost. If she and her fiancé had had an argument then it would account for her strange behavior. But why had she yelled? When he'd first heard the terror-filled scream, he'd rushed up the stairs and into Adelaide's room, fearing the worst, before he realized Kadie was still in his office. If she had been startled, what could have caused such a reaction? He really was beginning to wonder if Charlotte's ghost hadn't followed Kadie and Maysha after all.

Ever since Kadie had appeared with Charlotte's journal, his life had been very different—strange and unnatural. He'd never seen Adelaide act in such an eccentric manner, and he wondered at his own bizarre fascination with solving the mystery of the fire. It wasn't like him to get caught up in something like this, but he felt certain Aunt Charlotte's disappearance was no accident.

"Daddy?" Zaza's cheery voice broke through his thoughts, and he glanced up into his daughter's smiling face. "Can we take Kadie and Maysha camping on our beach tonight? Please? They've never camped on a beach before," she added, sounding shocked.

"Oh . . ." Kadie jumped in. She laughed. "That sounds like fun, Zaza, but Maysha and I don't have any camping gear."

The little girl shrugged. "We have plenty, silly. We can see the baby seals, and it's a full moon, so we can do a moonlight hike! You'll never get another chance again! You've got to go!"

Kadie caught her lower lip between her teeth and turned to Logan for support.

He grinned. "Why not, Kadie?" he asked.

Her mouth fell open uncertainly before she turned to consult Maysha. "Well . . . ?"

"It's an experience everyone who visits the Pacific Coast needs. It won't take long to set up camp, and I have a couple of tents and plenty of sleeping bags," Logan encouraged.

Kadie turned to face him again and he smiled. He could see her eagerness. Her sister groaned and slumped in her chair. "Camping . . . ugh! We have a perfectly good motel room waiting for us tonight."

Beth laughed. "I'm with you. If God intended for us to sleep outdoors, He wouldn't have made us smart enough to build houses."

Zaza giggled and stuck her tongue out toward Maysha and Beth. Maysha poked her tongue out in return, and Zaza laughed before she turned pleading eyes toward Kadie. "Pleeeeeaaase, Kadie?"

Kadie laughed, glancing toward her sister.

"I don't even have to ask," Maysha replied. "You want to go. You can't dangle something like a camping trip in front of Kadie without her going gaga."

Kadie's eyes narrowed exasperatedly before she asked Logan, "Are you sure it won't be a bother?"

"Not at all. We haven't camped on our beach in a long time. I say it's about time, don't you, Zaza?"

Zaza nodded, and then she threw her arms around Kadie. "Yahoo!" she whooped. Kadie laughed and hugged the little girl before she bolted out of her arms. "I'll get the marshmallows and chocolate! We're going to have so much fun. Just wait!" Zaza yelled, running across the kitchen. She paused and turned back toward Maysha. "You're coming too, aren't you?"

Maysha shook her head. "Oh, no! No way! I'll go along for the ride, but I *will not* sleep on the ground. I haven't slept on the ground since girl's camp, and I don't plan on ever doing it again."

Beth laughed. "You're welcome to come back to the house, Maysha. We have plenty of room," she offered.

Zaza glanced worriedly at Kadie. "But you'll stay right, Kadie? You can have your very own tent. It's not scary. Promise."

"Yes, of course I'll stay," Kadie reaffirmed and laughed when Zaza shouted happily.

* * * * * * *

It didn't take Logan long to gather all the camping gear. The beach was a very short walk from the house, and he quickly set up both tents while Zaza, Maysha, and Kadie wondered along the moonlit beach searching for shells and crabs in the sand. The weather was warm, and a soft, salty breeze blew in across the water, teasing Kadie's long hair. She paused near the water's edge and brushed several strands of hair from off her face. She gazed up at the star-studded sky and then back across the water. The waves distorted the moonlight and several lights from nearby homes shimmered on the water.

"Beautiful, isn't it?" Logan moved behind her. His voice sent a pleasant shiver across her skin and she caught her breath, startled at his silent approach.

"It is," she agreed.

She turned to smile at him and when his dark eyes met hers, she blushed. He watched her for a long moment, a smile hovering on his lips. He took a tentative step toward her, and Kadie's eyes broadened expectantly.

"Are you coming, Daddy?" Zaza called.

Logan paused. His smile widened, and Kadie turned from his penetrating gaze, feeling breathless and shaken. *What is wrong with me?* She wondered.

"We're coming, princess," he called.

Zaza came rushing back toward them, her pigtails bouncing against her small shoulders. She grasped Kadie's hand in hers. "We have to go to the other beach. Come on." She tugged on Kadie's fingers impatiently. "Just wait till you see them! The mama seal lets me get real close 'cuz she knows that I'll never hurt them," she explained as she pulled Kadie along the sandy beach.

Kadie laughed. She liked the feel of Zaza's hand in hers, and she and Logan shared a knowing smile as Zaza continued to ramble on about school, toys, and everything else that was important to a six-year-old.

"Now we have to go through the forest," the little girl explained when they reached the edge of beach. "It's okay though 'cuz Daddy's with us and there aren't any bears."

Kadie smiled, and she and Maysha followed Logan and Zaza through the thick forest. They followed a narrow path through the trees, and the bright moonlight cast eerie shadows on the heavily vegetated forest floor. When they came out onto a second beach, moonlight bathed the sand, bleaching it almost bone-white. The view was beautiful, yet eerie, and Kadie wrapped her arms about herself.

Zaza was quick to lead the way toward the family of seals, and when they drew near, the mother seal barked a warning.

"Not too close now, Zaza, remember?" Logan cautioned quietly.

Kadie was amazed at the cute little seal pups with their bright eyes and soft, gray coats.

"Oh, look at them," Maysha cooed. "I want to just squish one."

"I told you you'd love them," Zaza whispered.

They didn't stay long, for fear of upsetting the mother seal, and it didn't take long for them to hike back toward their tents. Once back on Logan's beach, he built a large fire, and they sat around its comforting warmth and roasted marshmallows.

Kadie was amazed at the green flames that licked at the dry driftwood, and Logan was quick to explain, "The salt from the ocean creates the different colors."

"Wow," Maysha exclaimed, "this stuff could mess with your head."

They chuckled quietly just as Zaza yawned.

"I think maybe we ought to call it a night, huh?" he asked, grinning.

Kadie nodded and suppressed a yawn of her own. "I'm pretty beat."

"Same here," he replied and added, "I'll walk Maysha back to the house." He stood and brushed the damp sand from off his jeans, smiling at Zaza. "Let's get you tucked in first, princess."

Zaza hugged Maysha before she threw her skinny arms around Kadie's neck. "Good night, Kadie," she whispered. The little girl's hot breath brushed against Kadie's cold skin.

Kadie squeezed Zaza gently. "Good night, Zaza. I think maybe I'll tuck myself in too. I'm pretty tired."

Logan agreed with a nod. He tucked Zaza into the tent before he and Maysha returned to the house. Maysha waved and Kadie stood, brushing the sand from her clothes before she unzipped her tent and stepped inside. Slipping off her shoes, she slid into her warm sleeping bag and listened to the sound of the surf and the fire crackling. A shore bird called in the distance, and Kadie's eyes grew heavy.

"Sleep tight. Don't let the beach-bugs bite." Zaza's voice cut through the ambience and the little girl giggled.

Kadie grinned sleepily and murmured, "Good night, Zaza."

Zaza giggled again, and the night grew quiet once more.

The day had been long, and Kadie felt both physically and emotionally exhausted. She sighed and listened with bated breath when she heard Logan's return. She heard the muffled sound of his sleeping bag zipper, and she smiled, wrapping her arms around her middle. The thought of Logan caused her stomach to flip-flop in a strange way. She enjoyed her time with him a bit too much. She'd scarcely met the man. She was acting like a fool, but she allowed herself a girlish grin before she closed her eyes. Tonight had been one of the best evenings she'd ever had, and Kadie was determined not to dampen her happiness with doubts and insecurities. She listened to the comforting sounds of the beach and happily drifted to sleep.

* * * * * * *

Kadie tossed violently in her sleep. She moaned and rolled over, twisting the sleeping bag around her body. She moaned again, trying to wake up, but she couldn't seem to pull her mind from the dream.

The raging inferno lit the sky and cast strange, demonic shadows dancing across the snow-covered ground. Kadie cried out and covered her head with her arms as darkness suddenly enveloped her. Frightened, she screamed as the ocean raged around her. Waves engulfed her body and she struggled desperately to keep her footing in the soft sand. Her body rolled with the swell and salty water filled her nose and mouth, burning her throat and searing her lungs.

She coughed and forced her trembling legs to carry her toward the moon-lit beach in the distance. Sobs shook her body as she crawled onto the damp sand and rolled to her back, desperately trying to catch her breath.

"Kadence."

A voice sounded above the din of the ocean, and knowingly, Kadie rolled to her knees. Charlotte. She rose weakly and turned, trembling, to face the jagged cliffs in the distance. Charlotte stood alone, high atop the precipice. Deep forest loomed behind her and the ocean raged below. The black waves broke on the yawning cliff face, sending fingers of clawing mist high into the air. Charlotte's nightdress glowed in the moonlight. Its length billowed like waves around her bare legs, and her dark hair rose behind her, dancing in the breeze.

"Charlotte," Kadie spoke her name as the ocean hissed against Kadie's legs. The water felt icy cold. "Charlotte!" she called, but her voice was lost on the wind. She suddenly felt desperate to reach her. "Please," she cried.

Charlotte turned to face her. The girl's nearly all-black eyes suddenly bore into hers. Terrified, Kadie stumbled, falling into the sand. Charlotte's hand rose toward her, beseeching, and she caught sight of Adelaide's pendant gleaming against the girl's pale chest.

Charlotte's mouth opened wide.

"Kadence . . . Kadie!"

Kadie's eyes grew large, and she swallowed when Charlotte called her name once again. Then without warning, the girl fell. Her body soared from the cliff and down into the dark water. She landed in the waves. Her nightgown floated out around her body as it tossed on the angry swells. Kadie screamed, but Charlotte's voice still rang in her ears. "Kadie . . . Kadie . . . ."

"Kadence!"

Kadie suddenly jerked awake.

Her eyes flew open and she stared wide-eyed at the top of her dark tent. Her breathing was shallow and labored, and sweat beaded thickly against her forehead.

"Kadence . . . ." A faint whisper floated around her tent, and she bolted upright, shivering.

A twig snapped outside near her tent and she held her breath. Her heart beat chaotically, painfully, against her ribs. A faint whimper and a soft thud sounded above the ocean waves.

"Zaza?" she whispered. A new, sudden, unexplainable fear gripped her.

Another loud snap sounded outside, and Kadie scrambled to her feet. She shoved her shoes on her feet and frantically unzipped the tent just as a shrill scream tore through the night. Kadie stumbled outside.

"Zaza?" she called, running forward.

She suddenly slammed into Logan's hard body, and she watched with fearful eyes when he stumbled slightly. Blood gushed from a wound on his head.

"Logan?" Kadie exclaimed as he spun around and ran toward the trees.

"Zahara!" he screamed.

Stunned, Kadie followed, pushing her legs to match his speed as he tore up the beach and into the black woods.

"Stop—Zaza—stop!" he screamed as he raced through the thick vegetation.

Kadie's breathing was shallow and labored as she tried to follow him. "Logan?" she yelled frantically.

Dense, thorny vegetation tore at her tender skin and scratched her face as she scrambled behind him, dazed. She couldn't keep up.

"Logan!" She choked on a scream when a dark figure loomed in front her. She was wrenched to the ground. Stunned, she fought blindingly, screaming as she tried to escape the hands clawing at her arms. Then without warning, fire shot up her shoulder and pain exploded behind her eyes.

"Help me," Kadie moaned before the darkness consumed her.

CHAPTER *Ten*

"Kadie, wake up! Kadence, open your eyes! Can you hear me?" Kadie groaned weakly, and she jerked when something soft and cold touched her forehead. She tried to force her eyes open, but the effort seemed too much. Pain consumed her, and her stomach lurched violently. Knowing she was going to vomit, she groaned again and rolled onto her stomach.

Her body heaved and warm hands closed about her thin, trembling shoulders. Pain exploded behind her eyes.

"Oh," she murmured as she spit the foul tasting bile from her mouth. Her eyes fluttered open, and she tried to sit up.

"Take your time," Logan whispered close to her ear.

She sat up weakly. "Logan?" she whispered and her eyes widened slowly when she caught sight of his blackened eye and the large jagged cut running from his forehead into his hairline.

He placed a cold, wet patch of moss against her head. "Is that better?" he asked, worry carved in the lines of his dirty face.

A cool breeze brushed across her body, and she looked around her, confused. Hundreds of tall trees, swaying gently with the breeze, surrounded the small clearing where she and Logan sat. The spongy ground beneath her soaked wetness through her clothes, and her eyes narrowed.

"Logan, where are we?" she whispered. She raised a hand to her throbbing head. "Where's Zaza?"

Logan shook his head. "They have her! They took Zahara," he replied between tightly clenched teeth then pushed the cold, moss compress against Kadie's left temple.

She winced and brushed his hand away. "Who? What's going on?"

Logan scowled and moved away. He stood and raked his hand through his already disheveled hair. "Senator Jukes. They took her and they left this." he replied, pulling a folded note from his front pocket.

Feeling shaky and weak, Kadie leaned forward to grasp the note. "I don't understand."

"I don't know where we are, Kadie. We aren't in the woods near my house anymore. I came back to consciousness right as the men who attacked us were taking off in a helicopter. I don't know what happened after they knocked me unconscious, but they must have transported us to these woods and left us here. They drugged us. You . . . you have a needle mark on your arm," he went on roughly. "Zaza . . . ." His voice cracked.

Kadie glanced down at her arm. "They took Zaza?" Her mind was numb. She felt stunned. She opened the note and tried to focus her eyes as she read the hastily scrawled words:

> If you ever want to see your daughter again, I suggest you stop meddling in the past. Leave well enough alone. It would be a real shame if this illustrious career of yours suddenly disappeared, or if your family met with a sudden series of accidents. Oh yes, we even have people in New York. We know all about you. You have a lot to lose, Counselor. We have given you and your girlfriend some time to consider your choices. Choose carefully or you will never see your little girl again. Perhaps spending a few days hiking out of these mountains will give you time to decide what is really important in your life.

Dumbfounded, Kadie suppressed a shudder. "They're *crazy*," she breathed as Logan grasped the note. The blood drained from her face, and her stomach churned again.

Logan folded the note with agitated hands and shoved it back inside his pocket. "Yeah!"

The depth of their situation was finally beginning to break through the cloudy haze that surrounded her mind, and she squeezed her eyes shut. The Jukes family had dumped her and Logan deep in the wilderness. Their only hope of saving Zaza was to find their way out.

Logan swore and knelt in front of Kadie. He reached out a large hand and placed it against her cheek. "How are you feeling? Are you okay?"

His hand dropped from her cheek, and he grasped her upper arm tenderly. He rubbed his finger against a slight bump under the skin. She glanced down and noticed some bruising around the puncture mark.

"I don't know what they used to knock us out, but it seemed to keep you under a lot longer. You aren't experiencing any numbness? Chest pain?" he asked.

She shook her head mutely.

"Kadie—"

"I'm fine, Logan," she whispered, "just a little nauseated."

"An effect of whatever they gave you, no doubt," he muttered angrily.

"It's passing."

"How's your head?" he cut in. "Keep this against it. It will help." He placed the wet wad of moss against her head once more and she reached up to hold it in place.

"You look awful. Are you okay?"

He grimaced and nodded. "I'm fine. It looks worse than it really is. I don't give a . . . I need to find my daughter." His teeth ground together, and he inhaled deeply. His nostrils flared.

Kadie reached out and tentatively touched his swollen eye. He grasped her fingers and squeezed them.

"What happened?" she asked. "I heard a noise and I followed you. But I can't remember anything else."

She shook her head, feeling muddled and disoriented. What had they given her? The thought scared her. She couldn't remember anything beyond chasing Logan into the woods.

"Someone attacked me before I was awake, but they didn't quite knock me unconscious. I heard Zaza scream, and I ran after them. That's when they attacked us in the woods. There were three of them, but I couldn't see their faces. That's all I remember. I came back to consciousness when the chopper was lifting off the ground. I couldn't even get a good look at the pilot. I found the letter in my front pocket. You've been out for a while. You can't know how relieved I was when you finally started mumbling. You were too still for too long. Are you sure you're doing all right?"

"I'm fine, really, Logan. I'm just a little foggy. I never could handle anything stronger than an aspirin . . . you know, 'just say no' and all," she murmured.

His eyebrows rose uneasily, and Kadie shook her head, dazed. "Really, I'll be fine. Where did they take Zaza? Do you know where we are? How far do we have to go to get back to town? And why would they just leave us here? " she asked. Her pulse accelerated as she pondered her questions.

How would they get out of these woods? What if the Jukes' men were still around, watching them? She glanced about her and grasped her rolling stomach as another wave of nausea threatened to erupt. She took a deep breath and looked around more slowly. The long grass in the meadow was bent at odd angles. A soft depression in the ground marred the beauty of the earth where the helicopter had landed.

Her eyes fell back toward Logan, and she read the rage in his expression as he answered her questions. "I don't where we are—and Zaza . . ." He swore, and Kadie winced. She noticed the rage building in his eyes. He breathed deeply and calmed a little. "We'll just have to take their word for it and head north until we find some help."

Kadie's fear for Zaza weighed heavy on her mind, and she grasped her churning stomach. What had they done with the little girl? How could they take her? She would be confused and terrified. The thought brought hot tears rushing to her eyes, and she watched Logan pace back and forth. Her heart contracted. Then she suddenly thought of Maysha and Beth.

"Maysha . . . and Beth, and Adelaide, do you think . . . ?" she voiced her fears.

"I don't know. We need to get out of here as soon as possible. All we can do now is get out of these woods," he answered gruffly.

"Logan," Kadie reached for him, wishing to offer comfort somehow.

He stopped pacing and grasped her hand. Emotions showed plainly in his dark eyes. "I have to get my baby girl back and when I do . . . ." His teeth ground together. His jaw clenched.

"Let's go then," she pressed.

"Are you sure you can?" He turned tormented eyes her way. "You were out for so long."

She stood, feeling somewhat wobbly, and Logan helped to steady her on her feet. Her legs were numb and tingly. She took a tentative step and stumbled backwards. Logan caught her abruptly, stabilizing her with a hand against the small of her back.

She laughed tersely. "This is why I steered clear of drugs in high school."

Logan grimaced.

"Just give me a minute." She shrugged out of his hold. She inhaled deeply, filling her lungs with fresh air, and stood straighter. After another long pause she asked, "Which way is north?"

* * * * * * *

Kadie's legs ached and her feet felt swollen and sore. She and Logan had been walking through heavily vegetated forest for several hours. Her stomach growled, and she clamped an arm about her midriff. The effects of the drugs she had been administered left her stomach feeling weak and unsettled. She caught Logan's worried eye several times throughout the day, but she had forced a smile. The walking was not easy. The thick undergrowth and slippery moss made traversing through the ancient rainforest tiring, and thick, prickly vines tangled with their ankles as they crossed several immense meadows.

Her mind filled with worry. What was happening back in town? Where was Zaza? What had the Jukes done to Maysha, Beth, and Adelaide? She closed her eyes. *Maysha . . .* she thought numbly. She didn't want to think about her sister. Maysha was all she had left. She was her sister, her confidante, and most important, she was Kadie's very best friend. If the Jukes men had gone back to the house, Kadie knew Maysha's temperament would not let her remain quiet. What would happen then? She grimaced, and her thoughts turned to Zaza with her happy, wide, toothless grin.

Kadie knew Logan was nearly out of his mind with worry. He had hardly spoken as they had traversed across the vast wilderness. What was he thinking? How could she help comfort him? Her own worry over the little girl and her fate was nearly overwhelming. What would it be like for Logan? She moaned softly and tried to concentrate on her feet. She had fallen more than once during the day, and she didn't want to risk any more unnecessary bruises or delays. The forest surrounding them was beautiful, but the thick trees and endless craggy rocks left her feeling undoubtedly discouraged.

The Jukes had left her and Logan stranded in the forest with nothing but the clothes on their backs and thankfully, the shoes on their feet. Kadie was very grateful she'd taken time to put her shoes on before she'd rushed from the tent. As it was, Kadie realized that they would probably not make it out of the mountains before nightfall and the thought left her feeling more depressed.

* * * * * * *

Logan tried to focus on listening to the sounds of the woods. He knew the sounds of wildlife would help him discover where they were. He didn't know how close they were to the ocean or if they were near any towns. He could not hear the surf, and the birds calling from within the trees did not sound at all like shore birds. Several high ledges surrounded them, making distant visibility impossible.

He heard the familiar warble of a wren, hidden among the forest understory, and the hooting call of a grouse resonated across the mountain meadow. The sounds of the forest were familiar to him, but they gave him little comfort. They'd been hiking through the woods for hours without any signs of humanity. No trails, no signs, nothing but the sun to guide their way, and even following the sun was difficult when they entered large areas of old-growth forests.

He felt frustrated. He was lost. He didn't know how long it would take to get out of the mountains. His teeth ground together at the thought of Senator Jukes and his son. When he managed to get his hands on those men . . . He shook his head. He was not a violent man, but the thought of Zaza in the hands of those monsters nearly killed him. How dare they take his daughter! What had they done with her? He knew his little daughter was scared. The thought of her frightened, alone, and crying made his heart tear.

He took a deep breath and clenched his hands into fists, trying to control his chaotic emotions. He stepped around a clump of spiny, wild blackberry bushes. He couldn't think about Zaza. He had to remain calm and in control. The only way to save his girl was to get out of these blasted mountains and find Senator Jukes as quickly as he could.

"Oh! Ouch," Kadie mumbled, pulling Logan from his thoughts.

He turned just as she stumbled over a moss-covered log. "Kadie!" He stepped back toward her.

She frowned. "Yes, just clumsy."

She stood and wiped the dirt and dead leaves from off the knees of her jeans. She looked exhausted, but she smiled wanly.

"I'm sorry," she breathed.

"Don't be. Are you okay? Do you need to stop?" he asked, sounding terse.

Kadie winced. "No, I don't. I'm fine."

"Kadie, I'm sorry—really," he apologized. "I'm just—"

"I know. I feel the same way."

"Do you need to rest?" he asked. His eyes traveled the length of her fatigued body, and he reached out slowly to place his hand against her soft cheek.

She shook her head. "No, I don't. We need to keep going," she replied.

He nodded and took the lead once again. A frown marred his face as he glanced toward the sky. Deep down he'd hoped that it would take only a few hours to reach help, but as evening drew near, he realized just how dire their situation really was. They had no survival gear, no food, and no way to ignite a fire. He didn't even have his wallet or his keys. They had nothing they could use to survive the elements. He understood that he and Kadie would need to stop soon.

He needed to take some time to evaluate their situation and better prepare himself and Kadie against the elements to avoid the risk of hypothermia. They had to find a good food source and clean water. Kadie and he couldn't hike for hours with no way to restore their depleted energy levels. He was quickly coming to respect the effort that it was going to take to hike out of the woods. Senator Jukes had said a few days, and apparently he had meant a few days. The thought caused Logan's blood to boil.

As a young man, he'd experienced several cross-country treks into the Olympics with his grandfather and Jace. He knew, given Washington's varied terrain, he could expect intense elevation gains and losses. There was a chance they would have to cross over high-alpine or sub-alpine areas where there would be very little source of food or shelter. They'd be exposed to the elements and cold, and as much as he wanted to rush headlong and find Zaza, he knew that if he didn't consider his and Kadie's safety, they wouldn't have much of a chance to rescue his daughter. They would die in the mountains if they weren't careful and smart.

Logan did, however, consider that he was lucky in a way. There probably wasn't an easier place for wilderness survival than the Pacific Coast. This time of year they'd be able to survive on the vegetation in the forest. The woods contained a variety of edible plant life, and he and Kadie could collect and eat what they could along their way.

When they stopped for the night, he could probably dig for edible roots. It wouldn't be as nourishing as meat, but without traps or a way to create fire . . . He inhaled deeply. That was one scout badge he had not honestly earned. He'd cheated. He'd never learned to start an adequate fire without matches.

"Just a minute," he heard Kadie call and he paused abruptly.

Kadie stopped at a rocky outcropping of metamorphic rock. She squatted and Logan could tell by the expression that flitted across her weary face that she was stiff and sore. He stepped closer as she rummaged through a small pile of broken rock. She found a rock about the size of her hand then tested the edge of the stone against her palm.

"This will work," she said, holding the rock high for Logan to see.

His eyebrows creased, confused, and she rushed to explain, "I'm assuming we're going to be here for the night. We can use this to cut pine boughs to stay warm. I wanted to get it now, just in case I can't find one later on."

Logan nodded. Apparently he was not the only one with survival on his mind. He was also impressed. He wouldn't have thought of that. "That's excellent." He studied their surroundings. "Listen—let's stop here for a bit. We need to rest. What do you think?" he asked.

Without answering, Kadie sat on the nearest boulder.

His legs felt stiff and sore as he sat next to her. He stared out toward a large meadow below them. It felt good to rest.

* * * * * * *

Kadie's mouth felt parched and gritty, and she licked her dry, chapped lips. She was thirsty. She hoped they crossed a stream soon. She glanced up at Logan as he sat next to her. His body heat radiated through his T-shirt, and she caught the mild scent of his aftershave. The beginnings of a dark beard shadowed his jaw, and he ran his hand absently across his chin. He stared out across the mountain, down toward the meadow in the distance. A herd of black-tailed deer grazed on the tall, lush grass.

The view was amazing, beautiful in fact, but discouraging. She sighed and wished she could lean her weary body against his. Her thoughts turned to Maysha and Zaza. What was happening to them?

"You're right about one thing," Logan spoke. "We're going to be here for the night, and I hope that I'm wrong, but we could be here for a few more as well. We need to get out of this lowland forest and up higher. I need a better idea of our location. If I knew where we were, we could get out a lot faster."

The thought of hiking higher left Kadie's legs feeling like gelatin. She nodded just as her stomach growled. Logan glanced down at her, and she smiled sheepishly. His brows knit in concern, and she laughed.

"I was thinking about the s'mores we ate last night," she blurted out.

Sadness swept over his features and Kadie bit down hard on her bottom lip, wishing she hadn't brought up the s'mores. *That was stupid*, she admonished. She knew he was worried about Zaza, and so was she. She couldn't imagine the mind-set of someone who could take another's child so callously.

He remained silent for a moment before he spoke, "We need to consider our situation. We have nothing for survival. We need to slow down and try to collect as much food as possible before nightfall. We also need to find a clean water source and find suitable shelter." He smiled at Kadie, then added, "Pine boughs will be perfect for keeping us warmer, and we're going to be cold, I'm afraid," he finished.

Silently, she reached into her pocket. She pulled out a small handful of dandelion leaves, a few wild blueberries, and some small strawberries. A few green leaves were smeared with sticky, blue juice. She held her palm out to Logan with an awkward smile. "I tried not to crush the berries."

His face twisted thoughtfully. "Have you done this before?"

She shrugged. "You'll be surprised at how creative I can get when I'm hungry."

Logan chuckled a little stiffly, and Kadie joined in. It felt good to laugh.

"Nice little salad you have there," he replied halfheartedly.

"My parents used to take Maysha and me camping as kids. One summer my dad bought an edible wild plant guide. He and I came up with all sorts of crazy salads that year. I don't think my mom and Maysha will ever forgive him for that summer."

"I bet not," Logan paused. "Tell me about your parents."

Knowing he was attempting to keep his mind from Zaza, Kadie obliged. "My mom and dad were great. Maysha and I came later in their life," she explained. "Mom wasn't able to have children, then one day when she was in her mid-thirties, she was miraculously pregnant with me. Maysha come less than two years later. Both my parents were educators. Dad was a professor of biology, and my mom taught high school physics. They were both science nuts."

"And you love history?" Logan's brow rose.

She nodded. "Dad used to laugh and say I must have been switched at birth." She paused for a moment, lost in the happy memories of her childhood before she went on slowly, "Mom died when I was twelve. She was diagnosed with breast cancer. Dad raised both Maysha and I alone, then last year he had a stroke. He hung on for a few months."

Logan's small smile faded and he whispered, "I'm sorry."

"Dying was a blessing for Dad—Mom too. At the time it was hard to see that. Dad had a tough time raising two, hormonal, teenage girls. I always thought he'd remarry, but he never did. Sometimes I wish he had. My parents were both wonderful people, and I miss them terribly. Maysha and I are all each other have left. We . . . ." She paused as emotions rushed to the surface.

She was so worried about Maysha. She couldn't lose her sister too, and she felt utterly helpless. What was happening back in town? Logan seemed to read her thoughts, and he reached out to grasp her hand in his. His large, calloused hand felt comforting against Kadie's cold fingers.

"She'll be fine. Senator Jukes . . . he . . . well, Maysha's tough—spunky." Logan tried to offer comfort.

"But that's what worries me. She doesn't know when to keep her mouth shut. You've seen that. What if she makes them angry? I couldn't live without her, and I'm so sorry about Zaza. Why are they doing this?" she whispered. Tears pooled against her long lashes and rolled down her cheeks. She swiped at them angrily. "If I'd never come . . . I was so *stupid*. If I hadn't brought that journal, you and you're family would be safe. Zaza wouldn't be gone and—"

"Whoa!" Logan cut her off. "Kadie, this is not your fault!"

"If I hadn't brought that journal and upset Adelaide, you're life would have gone on the same. You and I wouldn't be stuck in these mountains with Zaza missing!"

"Things are what they are. Your showing up with that journal had nothing—*nothing* to do with our current situation. If *anyone* is to blame then it's me. I provoked the senator. I knew what I was doing. The moment I saw Kenny's face, I knew I had to find the truth. I was a fool!"

She inhaled sharply. "Zaza . . . Will she . . .?" she whispered.

"All we can do is hope they keep their end of the bargain. I can't lose my temper yet. I have to stay focused, and we need to get out of these mountains, but we need to do it as safe as possible. There's no sense in dwelling on what might have been. That won't help us at all."

"Well, I guess we don't need to wonder whether or not Senator Jukes is responsible for the Clarke family's death," she replied mirthlessly.

"No, I guess we don't." Logan reached for her hand and squeezed her fingers before he stood. "I can see a marshy area up ahead. I'd like to follow the stream and find the water's source. We don't want to mess with bacteria. We can camp by the head of the spring, and it'll be a good place to finish that salad of yours."

CHAPTER *Eleven*

*D*arkness was quickly descending on the mountains, and the air was growing ever cooler. Kadie watched as Logan dragged a few extra pine boughs closer to their makeshift shelter. He propped the boughs against the edge of the small, double overhang they had discovered to create a more protected refuge. He tossed a few boughs onto the second shelf.

"That should do it," he murmured before he crawled in next to Kadie.

He sat on the pine bough carpet they had spread out across the dirt and pulled out a handful of small, white bulbs.

"Camas bulbs," he explained and Kadie eyed the potato-like tubers curiously.

She reached behind her and pulled out a large slab of pine bark. Her makeshift salad bowl held an assortment of dandelion leaves, a few more strawberries that she had collected by the stream, and a handful of wild blueberries.

"Not bad," Logan commented dryly as he threw his find into the mix.

Kadie slid two more curved slabs of bark out from behind her. She had washed the dirt and dried pine needles from off the wood the best she could in the stream, and Logan eyed her with a weary but appraising smile.

They ate their meager, vegetarian meal in silence. The quiet of the night stretched between them and Kadie grimaced when she stuck another bitter dandelion leaf in her mouth. "Needs salt," she suddenly blurted aloud.

Logan chuckled tersely, eating another camas bulb. "This is an acquired taste I think."

The tubers had a very woodsy taste, but the berries were sweet and delicious, and they left Kadie's stomach yearning for more. She determined to keep a better watch for more berries in the morning as they traveled. It was not much of a meal, but it put food in their stomachs, and Kadie could feel her energy expanding. The long hike on an empty stomach had taken a toll on her.

She watched Logan out of the corner of her eye as he ate. His eyebrows were creased in thought, and he leaned back against the stone. The silence stretched between them. She wanted to learn more about him, but she knew his thoughts were centered on Zaza. She stifled a yawn and leaned wearily against the uncomfortable, jagged wall. She adjusted her shoulders to find a more comfortable position, and when she glanced up, she was startled to see Logan watching her.

"So," he murmured. "Why are you marrying Robert?" he asked, his voice weary.

She was shocked by the unexpected question, and her eyes shot to his. She was unable to read his expression in the fading light, and she cringed when she felt the heat rise in her cheeks. She saw a flash of white teeth, and he laughed abruptly.

"It doesn't have to be light for me to see you blush. You blush easily—I like that. Tell me how you met him?" Logan encouraged.

"Why?" she inquired, confused.

Logan shrugged and frowned. "Like I said earlier, I need to keep my mind occupied. Please?" He encouraged.

"Well," Kadie answered self-consciously. "We met at a school function. It was teeth awareness day and—"

"Teeth awareness day?" Logan laughed.

"Yes," Kadie shrugged. "Robert was the residential dentist who visited the school."

"Oh—I see. And you fell in love while passing out fluoride tablets and floss."

Her lips twitched. "Sort of. At first he was . . . charming—sweet. We've been engaged for nearly a year, but well . . . well, last night I sort of . . ." She clasped her nervous stomach. "Well, I broke our engagement."

Logan sat silent for several long moments, and Kadie blushed. "Why?" Logan asked quietly.

Lifting her shoulders high, she answered, "We've grown too far apart. I don't believe he ever understood me," she hastened to explain. "He just isn't what I want. I really did enjoy being with him. He was a fantastic friend, but a terrible fiancé. He wouldn't have made me happy. Anyway, Maysha's right. He's far too . . . *stuffy*."

Logan's deep laughter filled their little cavern. "Really?" he chuckled. Then asked, "And what sort of man would make you happy?"

Kadie shrugged. Her heart beat against her chest, and she hoped he couldn't read how plainly he affected her. *You*, she thought, *you make me happy*. She bit her lip, and asked, "What about you? You said you were divorced?"

Logan nodded. "I am. Her name was Ashley Edmond. She was the daughter of a well-to-do judge in New York. She was beautiful, intelligent, spiteful, and spoiled. Her daddy gave her everything and anything she wanted. She loved the fast life. I let myself believe that a marriage between us would work. I don't think she wanted to get married to begin with.

"I think the only reason she finally agreed to a traditional marriage was because I'd have it no other way. Anyway, she left three months after Zaza was born. I didn't even have to contest custody. She just signed her over. Zaza and I have never heard or seen from her since. Last I heard she had moved to Paris with yet another boyfriend."

"That's so sad. How could anybody . . . ? Zaza is such a treasure. I can't imagine how a mother could leave their child for *anything*," Kadie replied, shocked.

Logan exhaled loudly. The mention of Zaza's name tore at her heart, and Kadie regarded him closely when he answered. "Truthfully, I believe it's better this way. It was the least selfish thing she ever did—leaving me with Zaza. Zaza has asked about her mother over the years, naturally, but Ashley . . . she'd only bring Zaza heartache." He groaned then added bitterly, "Of course if Zaza had stayed with Ashley, she wouldn't be missing right now." He ducked his head, glaring toward the ground.

"Logan . . . ." Kadie grew silent and watched Logan shake his head. His fists balled, and through the fading light, she saw the strain around his eyes and mouth.

"Why don't we try to get some sleep. I have a feeling we are going to have a long day tomorrow. I'm . . . uh—heading up to the top bunk," Logan spoke.

"Okay," she agreed as Logan crawled from underneath the small overhang. He stood, and his feet disappeared as he jumped to the second shelf. She hoped he'd stay warm enough. The second ridge, though just above her shelter, was much more exposed than where she sat, and she hoped the pine boughs would be enough to block the wind and chill. She closed her eyes and hoped morning would come soon.

* * * * * *

Charlotte lay face-down in the dark waters. The waves broke around her, tossing her body to and fro as if it were weightless. Her long hair flowed out in a fan-like plume, waving gently on the current. Thunder sounded from above, and black clouds collided, warring in the sky. Suddenly, Charlotte's body turned to face the sky, and Kadie stared down into her own likeness.

"No!" she screamed and jerked awake with a loud gasp.

"What is . . . *what*?" Logan's voiced sounded from overhead. Kadie heard a thud, and she cringed when Logan suddenly appeared on the ground next to her shelter. He groaned and rolled to his knees.

She bolted upright, breathing heavily as the nightmare dissipated. Logan's stunned eyes fell on her warily, and she took a deep, shuddering breath, wiping the dampness of perspiration from off her brow. "Just a dream . . . it was just a dream. I'm sorry," she whispered. "Are you . . . are you all right? Did you get hurt?"

Logan's tense shoulders slumped, relieved, and he rolled back onto the ground with a deep sigh. "Give me a heart attack." He raked a hand through his hair and glared toward the sky. "And, no, I'm fine," he finished.

"I'm sorry." Kadie took another calming breath before she rolled out from their makeshift shelter and stumbled into the coming dawn.

Birds chorused loudly from the trees. Their warbles and whistling tunes echoed off the basalt cliffs that surrounded them. The stream burbled, and she breathed in, relaxing as she inhaled the spicy scent of woods and damp earth. Her hands trembled, and she brushed her hair out of her face before she walked to the edge of the stream.

"What do you want, Charlotte?" she whispered into the dawn.

"Kadie?" Logan called from behind. The sound of his deep voice had a stabilizing effect on her jumbled nerves.

She shivered as she tried to dispel the emotions that haunted her then turned to face Logan with a forced smile. She caught her breath when he drew near. Thick stubble accented his strong jaw, and his disheveled hair stood in untidy tufts. *He's so handsome*, Kadie mused. *Why does he affect me this way?*

He grasped her shoulders when he reached her. "What's going on?"

"I'm fine. I had a nightmare, that's all."

He watched her intently before pulling her close, wrapping his strong arms around her thin shoulders. With a sigh, she leaned into his broad chest and relished the feeling of being near him. His warm embrace chased the frightening remnants of the dream from her mind. He held her for only a short moment before he pulled back and released her gently.

"Must have been some dream, huh?" He whispered.

"Mmm-hmm," she answered.

He moved to the edge of the stream, and she regarded him while he knelt and splashed a few handfuls of the frigid spring water across his face. He stood and stared out across the meadow. Kadie followed his gaze, and she felt dismayed when she noticed the dark clouds on the horizon. A breeze whispered across the tall grass. The swaying hemlocks and firs that surrounded them sighed softly.

"Besides suffering from nightmares, how are you feeling this morning?" Logan asked without taking his eyes off the meadow.

She cringed. "Better than yesterday. I'm sore, but I have my energy back," she responded. "Looks like rain?"

"Mmmm," he returned. "What do you say we rummage up a bit of breakfast before we head out? I'll dig up a few more camas bulbs to eat on the way. We need to get moving."

Kadie seasoned another tasteless camas root with a ripe, juicy blueberry. They ate their meager breakfast as they crossed a subalpine meadow. The breeze was chilly, and dark clouds smothered the sun, casting bleak shadows across the terrain. She glanced up at the sky and moaned. *Now it's going to rain*, she thought sardonically. The whole time she had been in Washington, she had seen nothing but blue skies and sunshine. It was ironic to Kadie that it would rain now. She popped another camas bulb in her mouth and grimaced.

"I don't think I'd make a very good caveman," she called to Logan.

He turned briefly and his mouth quirked. "Oh, yeah?" he answered darkly. Kadie could easily read his bad temper in the lines of his face.

"This naturalist diet grows old—fast. I miss my Ho-Ho's and potato chips." She attempted to tease, hoping to lighten his mood.

Logan smiled stiffly. "Yeah, well, I think my Neanderthal ancestors would be very disappointed with me. I can't even make a blasted fire."

"You mean they didn't teach a Neolithic course in law school?" she pressed with a small smile.

Logan suddenly swore and he turned to face her. "No, but I'm beginning to think they should have," he answered, all traces of humor gone.

Taken aback, Kadie's eyes widened and her mouth fell open. "Logan . . . ," she breathed. "I'm sorry. I didn't mean . . . ." She shook her head.

His eyes darkened, and he raked a hand through his hair. His jaw convulsed. He groaned, and she tried desperately to hide her sudden hurt. She closed her eyes for a second. She was a fool. She knew his thoughts centered on his daughter, and she had no business acting like a child. She lowered her eyes to the ground just as he suddenly gathered her in his arms. Shocked, she stiffened, and her breath left her lungs in a rush.

"Kadie, I'm sorry," he spoke gruffly. "I didn't mean to sound angry. Forgive me. I'm just . . . ." His fingers buried in her hair, and he pressed her face against his chest. Unsure, she slowly slipped her arms around his waist. His arms tightened around her.

"No, I shouldn't have—"

"You didn't do anything. I had no right to snap. We . . . Kadie, I don't know where we are. We have to get out of these blasted mountains, and *I don't know* where we are," he ground out. "I'm just frustrated. Forgive me, please. You didn't do anything wrong," his voice softened.

Feeling helpless and confused, she leaned against him. Her body relaxed, and she forced back a sudden wave of tears. He needed her to be strong, and she wouldn't give in to her frustrations. She had no words to comfort him. "It's okay," she whispered lamely.

He leaned his head against her brow, and she felt his rapid heartbeat. "I'm glad you're here. I think I'd go mad without you."

Kadie's lips parted, and she felt bereft when his arms suddenly dropped from around her. Their eyes met, and he licked his dry lips before he leaned in and pressed them to hers. Her breath caught as his lips explored hers for only a moment, and when he pulled back, he smiled a little. "Thank you," he whispered.

She inhaled deeply and placed a hand to her fluttering stomach. "I'm glad I'm here too," she answered before he smiled weakly and turned away.

With a pounding heart, she moved to follow.

* * * * * * *

They stepped across another glacial stream, pausing to take a drink before they entered the forest once again. Thick moss and Oregon oxalis painted the forest's understory and giant Sitka spruce reached for the sky. Kadie watched the ground, taking an interest in the various fungi and little, odd pink flowers. When she noticed several yellow banana slugs, leaving behind thick trails of gleaming slime, she grimaced a little. Her feet snapped a twig, hidden underneath the thick vat of moss and lichen, and she gasped when she suddenly rammed into the back of Logan's firm back.

"Sorry," Kadie murmured self-consciously. "I—"

"Shhh," Logan turned to steady her, and he raised a finger to his lips.

Her brow furrowed and he pointed ahead. Her gaze followed his direction, and she squinted through the dark haze toward a spiny patch of raspberry brush. She held her breath and grasped Logan's forearm tightly when the head of a very large brown bear appeared in the thicket.

"Let's go," she whispered hoarsely.

Logan pulled her hand into his and they backed up slowly. Kadie turned and she and Logan made a wide perimeter around the bear. She focused on breathing and glanced behind her. Logan caught her eye, and he nodded knowingly.

"I don't like bears," she alleged.

"I doubt he would have bothered us if we had stuck to our original course, but it probably wouldn't be the best gamble to make either," he added.

They stopped around midday for a short break, and Kadie's stomach growled. Her feet ached with weeping blisters, and she breathed deeply as they sat on a flat boulder, overlooking a deep gorge. Basalt cliffs rose high into the sky, their peaks disappearing into the low, black clouds. Thunder rumbled in the distance, and several rain drops fell from the sky.

"I think we can assume we're in for more than a slight drizzle," Kadie commented, eyeing the somber clouds.

Logan looked up and nodded. "We probably shouldn't stop here for long. We'll be better protected down in the gorge where the trees are thicker."

Her gaze wandered across the mountains. "I can't believe how diverse this place is."

"The different levels of precipitation means a lot of different habitats are crowded into one area. I'm assuming we're in the Olympics."

She nodded absently, and Logan stood. He pointed down toward the gorge. "Let's get off this ridge and down there. We're going to need to find some cover before this storm hits. Hopefully it doesn't last too long. We can cross this meadow and descend over there." He offered his hand to Kadie.

She took his proffered hand, and he helped her stand. Thunder growled again, and without a moment's notice the sleeting rain suddenly burst from the clouds.

"Come on, let's go!" He ran across the meadow.

Kadie ducked her head against the frigid rain and followed close behind, careful to avoid tripping on rocks and branches hidden in the tall grass. Her legs felt wooden as she tried to jump over a dead log. Her feet landed on the wet grass and she slipped. Her arms flayed as she tried to steady herself, then suddenly a bird flew directly in front of her. Its loud warble pierced the quiet of the mountains. She cried out, and with no hope of regaining her tenuous balance, she fell backward over the large log with a quiet, "humph."

"Kadie!" Logan called. Turning, he rushed back toward her.

Shaking her head, she rolled onto her knees and stood. "Dumb bird," she muttered.

Logan caught her eye and a small smile touched his lips. "Are you okay?" he asked, humor laced his voice.

"I'm fine," Kadie mumbled. "Nothing broken but my pride."

His brow knit and his smile grew before his eyes abruptly widened. "Hey, where did that bird come from?" he asked, glancing around in the tall grass.

Her brow furrowed, and her expression twisted curiously. She pointed to the spot where the bird had first launched its air attack. "There." She pointed.

Logan stepped carefully toward the area she directed and pushed the tall grass aside. "Ah-hah!" he called triumphantly. He pulled four small eggs from a nest hidden in the vegetation.

Kadie's lips turned down and she eyed the brown, speckled eggs with a dawning mixture of disgust and horror. "And we are going to boil them—how?" she asked sarcastically.

Logan's eyebrows rose. "Trust me—your body will thank me later."

"No—I don't think it will."

His smile faded. "It's amazing what you'll enjoy when your body is literally starving for calories. You might find them fairly appetizing."

"Doubtful—very doubtful," she murmured.

"Let's get out of this rain. All we need is a nice bout of hypothermia to along with our eggs." Logan ducked his head against the rain and took up the lead once again.

They were wet and chilled by the time they reached the edge of the meadow. They rushed into the woods and took cover at the base of a giant Sitka. Cold rain water ran down Kadie's neck, and she shivered.

"We can wait out the worst of it here, but this won't do for long," Logan spoke as he sat next to her.

He wrapped his thick arm about her trembling shoulders and pulled her closer to his side. Wearily, Kadie leaned her head against his chest and listened to his ragged breathing and his quick heartbeat. Her heart beat fast as his arm tightened about her. She enjoyed Logan's nearness a bit too much. Robert's touch had never made her heart race the way Logan's did. She sighed then suppressed a cold shiver, trying to pull her thoughts away from Logan. She couldn't allow her mind to get caught up in romantic daydreams. She knew her feelings for Logan were genuine, but now . . . well, now was not the time to dwell on them. She needed to focus on surviving.

She heard the soft sound of rain as it fell against the trees and ferns that surrounded them, and she let her eyes wander toward the tops of trees. She was amazed at the curtain of moss hanging from the immense branches of the giant tree. Ferns grew along the branches, and Kadie pointed toward them, impressed.

"I've never seen that," she spoke. "Look at that."

Logan followed her gaze. "The moss helps germinate the spores. You'll see that fairly often in these temperate rain forests."

"This place really is amazing. Too bad I have to see it under these circumstances," Kadie added.

His eyes narrowed. "If this rain keeps up much longer, we're going to have to find dry shelter. We can't keep going in this. I just hope we can get in a few more hours. We need to get out of these woods." Kadie could hear the frustration in his words. "You're not too cold are you?" he asked.

"No," she murmured.

She wasn't looking forward to spending another night in the woods. She was impatient to reach help. Everything depended on her and Logan getting out of the mountains. They could do nothing for Zaza as long as they were lost in the woods, and the thought made her jaw tighten. She glanced up at the patch of dark sky visible through the trees.

Growing up in Utah, where the rain was not nearly as common

as in the Northwest, she loved the sound of pouring rain. Now, however, the sound left her feeling frustrated. Like Logan, she hoped they could cover more ground today. Her worry for Zaza and the rest of their family weighed heavy on her mind.

"Here," Logan broke through her thoughts. He handed her two speckled eggs.

Kadie's expression twisted into disgust and she watched mutely when he pulled his arm from around her shoulder and cracked an egg into his mouth. Her stomach churned, and she suppressed a gag as she watched him swallow. He ate the second, tossing the shells into the ferns.

"I really . . . ." She held the eggs out to Logan, but he closed her fingers around the eggs and pushed her hand away gently.

"Don't think about it."

Her face twisted in disgust as she eyed the eggs in her hands. The shells radiated warmth and her stomach rejected the idea with an aching twist. "No—really. I'll go dig up some more roots or something."

He smiled. "It's not that bad. You need the energy. Besides, the thought of doing something is often worse than the reality. Come on!"

She knew he was anxious to get moving again, so she took a deep breath before cracking the egg against her teeth. She suppressed a retch as the thick, slimy ooze slid down her throat. "*Eh* . . . ."

"One more."

With a groan, she cracked the second egg and deftly swallowed its contents. She tossed the shells into the tall grass and shuddered. "Yuck! Honestly—" she gagged. "Next time I'll just die first."

"See, not bad, huh?" He looked up toward the top of the trees and Kadie glared at him. "We can't stay in this. We need to find drier shelter, are you ready?"

She stood on stiff legs. "Yes, but those eggs had better give me the energy you promised."

Logan chuckled before he took the lead. They pushed through the thick forested area, working their way down toward the gorge they'd noticed while sitting atop the ridge. The rain caused an eerie vapor to rise from the ground. The forest sounds were muffled and distorted. Walking through the mist-shrouded forest was an odd sensation, and it left Kadie feeling disoriented and on edge. The wet ferns grew in dense patches, making their progress through the forest slow. The barrier of vegetation tugged at their ankles and soaked wetness through their already wet jeans. The wind caused the trees to sway and groan, and the scuttle of small rodents seemed amplified in the thicket.

As they approached an area where a rugged cliff rose, cutting through the forest, Logan slowed and turned toward the right fork. The rain was finally letting up, and the trees were thinning. The going looked much easier, and with a sigh, Kadie followed just as a movement on the edge of the left fork caught her eye. She turned warily, and then gasped. A woman stood among the trees, and the mist swirled about her in snake-like tendrils. Kadie blinked hard. When she glanced up again, the woman was gone. The ethereal mist crawled along the forest floor, and Kadie stepped closer, her eyes wide.

Thunder grumbled above them, muffled by the dense overhead foliage, and she shuddered. It had to be her imagination. Surely she had not seen anyone. She moved closer toward the spot, drawn by some unexplainable force. Charlotte? She voiced silently.

"What is it?" Logan called.

She spun around and her hands fluttered nervously. He watched her as she shuddered. "Nothing . . . it's nothing. I saw a deer or something." Then, "Logan, can we go this way?" The words burst from her lips.

Kadie couldn't explain what was going on. I am crazy, she thought wildly. Yet somehow, she knew that she and Logan needed to follow the left fork. She looked to the trees again, almost fearfully. She watched the forest for any sign of unnatural movement with wide, almost expectant eyes. She heard Logan's soft steps behind her.

"I suppose we can," he answered. "Why?" he asked.

She turned to face him. She hoped he couldn't read her bewildered expression. If she told him she was seeing apparitions in the mist, he'd probably abandon her in the woods.

"I don't know," she answered. "It's just a feeling, I guess."

Logan studied the right fork and then the left with narrowed eyes. He shrugged. "Why not."

Kadie felt hesitant as they approached the area of forest where she was certain she'd seen Charlotte. The mist seemed thicker in this area of the woods, and Kadie shivered, wondering if she were nuts. She had to trust she was making the right choice in following her strange premonition. The right fork had looked much easier and much less sinister. Logan led the way cautiously. The mist pressed in, suffocating, and she wondered if she ought to change her mind.

CHAPTER *Twelve*

The thick mat of moss and vegetation made traversing through the woods difficult. Several large rocks were camouflaged beneath the muddy, organic carpet, and Kadie slipped several times on the uneven surface. They hiked in silence for several hours, and her legs felt weak with exhaustion. Despite the rough terrain, Logan kept up a brisk pace that taxed Kadie's muscles.

They stuck to the base of the cliff as well as they could, but as the gorge narrowed and steepened, they slowed in order to negotiate their path over the large, lichen-covered boulders, and Logan turned to help her over several rougher areas. The basalt stone was coarse and jagged, and Kadie cringed when she slipped and caught her knee on the edge of hard stone. She hissed in pain. Logan paused and glanced back worriedly.

"Are you hurt, Kadie?" he asked, coming to her side.

His ragged breathing matched hers, and she looked ahead, frustrated. The canyon was littered with more jagged boulders. It was sapping all their strength to climb the massive stones. Logan's eyes mirrored her own frustrations.

"Maybe this wasn't such a good idea." Kadie's head hung dejectedly.

"For all we know, the other direction could have been the same or worse," Logan muttered.

He sat next to Kadie. His shoulders slumped, and they sat in silence for several moments while they rested their burning muscles and caught their haggard breaths.

"Do you think we should turn around?" she questioned after several silent moments.

"Turn around where?" he asked. "We were just as lost before. Besides, there has to be a way down off this ridge, and I'd hate to turn around now. We're getting closer to the top."

"It's probably a sheer drop to the ground," Kadie muttered, discouraged.

"Could be, but I don't want to turn around until we know for sure."

She studied the distant horizon. The rugged path grew steeper, unbelievably more rugged, and narrow. Her shoulders slumped. *I think you're trying to kill us, Charlotte*, she thought jadedly. Why had they come this way? Taking the left fork had obviously been a mistake. What had she been thinking? She was clearly off her rocker if she were seeing apparitions in the fog and following crazy hunches. Her dreams were obviously creating some sort of paranoia that was playing itself out during daylight hours, causing her to imagine Charlotte's image.

Kadie moaned internally. If they reached the top and had to turn around then they had wasted several precious hours, and it would be her fault. It would be dark in a few short hours, and they had yet to find another *living* soul in these mountains. They hadn't crossed a trail or a sign or anything to indicate they were walking in the right direction. She felt frustrated to the point of being angry, and she glared down at her feet.

"What if we get to the top and it goes nowhere? We will have wasted so much time," she spoke angrily. "I'm so sorry."

"It doesn't matter, Kadie. It isn't your fault. Besides, this goes high—higher than we've climbed yet. Maybe we can get a good view of the area. If we can see a city or a town, then it's been worth every bit of effort." He patted her shoulder before he glanced up the narrow canyon. "We're going to have to take our time and go slow. The moss on these rocks is very slippery. One wrong move and we could easily break our legs, if not our necks."

Kadie followed his gaze and cringed. With her luck she would slip off a boulder and break her neck. She stood. "Let's go," she moaned dispassionately.

Logan nodded wearily and stood, taking the front. He was careful to choose the safest path as they ascended the steep, rugged mountain. Little vegetation grew on the rugged ridge. Only short bushes and moss seemed to grow in the narrow cracks between the craggy stones and loose rock. Kadie glanced behind them. The forest below was shrouded in mist, and she swallowed her fear. The sight was eerie and grave. The view left her feeling even more on edge.

The hairs on her arms stood on end. She felt as though unseen eyes watched her as she stared at the mist that rose and swirled, high above the tree tops. A breeze stirred the loose strands of her hair about her face and she brushed at them absently as she studied the thick cloud of haze. Human-like shapes seemed to hide in the swirling mist, and she shuddered again. *Get a hold of yourself. Charlotte's ghost is not real.*

She tore her eyes away and turned back to follow Logan. She pulled her thoughts from ghosts and ghouls to focus on crossing the rough terrain safely. Logan slowed to give her time to catch up, and when she finally reached him, her breathing was labored and sweat beaded along her brow, despite the chilly air. She slumped on the rock next to Logan, weak from exertion.

"Do you want to wait here while I go on up to the top to check things out?" Logan asked, touching her back gently.

Kadie glanced down toward the mist shrouded forest and shuddered.

"No," she replied. She didn't want to be left alone at all. "I'll be fine. I just—"

"Shhh!" Logan cut her off. His body tensed and he turned toward the top of ridge, listening.

"What is—"

"Listen," he breathed.

Her heart picked up pace, and she turned toward the ridge, listening. They waited for several minutes, and her brows creased in confusion. What exactly were they listening for? She strained her ears and tried to hear past the rush of blood pulsating in her head. Logan's breathing was shallow and his body remained tensed as if waiting to spring. Suddenly several shrill yips sounded in the distance, and Kadie sucked in a sharp, frightened breath.

"Wolves?" she whispered.

Logan shook his head slowly. "No, I don't think so."

More barks sounded in the distance, and she glanced at Logan, worriedly. "Coyotes, then?"

"Maybe, but there's only one. It doesn't sound quite like a coyote. I think—"

"Did you hear that?" Kadie's head shot up and her eyes grew large.

Another sound reached her ears, different and more resounding than the dog, but harder to distinguish. The sound came again, a bit louder than before.

"Logan, I heard someone. Someone calling," she whispered.

Logan shot to his feet, balancing his weight on the boulder. "Hey!" he called. "Hello! We need help! Help!" he yelled again.

"Help! Help us!" Kadie's voice joined Logan's.

Logan began climbing again, and with renewed energy, Kadie scrambled to follow. He continued to call as they hurried up the steep slope. Ignoring the burning in her lungs, she pushed herself to keep pace with Logan. The dog continued to bark in the distance. The sound bounced off the steep cliffs.

Soon they reached the top and with relief she realized it was not a steep drop off after all, but the descent looked treacherous. Giant, dump-truck-sized boulders led the way to a fog-shrouded forest at the bottom of the ridge. A fat layer of moss, lichen, and ferns covered the stones' surface.

The dog continued to bark and Logan called again, "Hello! Hello! We need help!" They listened for a moment before he looked to her anxiously. "Do you think you can manage this?"

"Yes." She nodded and swallowed hard.

"Keep a tight hold on me," he suggested, grasping her hand in his. "Let's hope there are campers nearby. That dog's only a quarter-mile or so away. "

"Do you think they can hear us?"

"I don't know. Whoever it was must have been at the bottom of this ridge for us to have heard them calling, but the dog's moving further away now. Let's hurry, but—just be careful."

Logan held tightly to Kadie's hand as they began their precarious descent down the ridge. The slick covering made negotiating their footing hard and slow. Below them, the dog continued to bark, and Kadie hoped they could reach someone soon. She wondered what she and Logan would do once they reached help. Senator Jukes had said he'd be in touch. What exactly had he meant? Did he expect Kadie and Logan to sit and wait once they found their way out of the mountains? Her stomach clenched at the uncertainty of their future.

She still couldn't quite conceive that Senator Jukes had dumped them in the wilderness and taken Zaza. The thought of the little girl caused a cold sweat to break across her balmy skin. What if they never made it out? What if she and Logan died in these mountains? What exactly was the Senator's plan then? She shook her head to clear her thoughts, and again she wondered if the continued yipping was truly a pet and not some coyote—or worse, a wolf.

She was certain she'd heard someone calling, and this time she was confident it was not a ghost or some crazy apparition she had dreamed up. Logan heard it too, and she hoped he was right about campers. They desperately need to get out of the mountains and back into Bremerton. She had to see Maysha. Her anxiety over her sister and Logan's little girl increased as the hours passed, and she knew Logan was even more worried about Zaza.

"Careful, Kadie," he cautioned as they worked their way down a house-sized boulder.

He held her hand tightly, but despite his support, her feet slid tenuously. She cringed as she regained her footing. "I can manage."

"Careful here." He jumped across a wide, gaping fissure in the rock and turned to help Kadie. She eyed the deep, yawning hole warily as he reached toward her. "Just jump, I'll catch you," he reassured.

Kadie took a deep breath and jumped across the crack. Logan caught her and kept a firm hold on her elbow as he steadied her. She glanced behind her and released a ragged breath before she moved past Logan.

"Can you still hear the dog?" she asked.

Suddenly, Kadie heard a soft thud. Logan swore and she spun around just in time to watch as he slipped off the edge of the giant boulder. He yelled as he disappeared into the dark fissure and Kadie's shrill scream echoed off the cliff walls.

"Logan!" She rushed to the edge and peered down. "Logan!" she called, her tone frantic.

Logan groaned, and relief washed over Kadie in waves. "Kadie . . . ?"

Stunned, her eyes broadened and she struggled to hear past the ringing in her ears. "Logan," she yelled. "Are you all right? Are you hurt?" Her voice echoed. He was sprawled in a strange angle on the floor of the yawning hole. He moaned and sat up then looked to Kadie. "Logan, are you hurt?"

He ran a hand through his hair and stretched his forearm tentatively. He swore beneath his breath.

"Logan, your arm! Are you okay?"

"Yes—I'm fine. Just bruised, I think. I landed on my arm the wrong way, but it's fine. "

He stood slowly and stretched his arm again. He looked up toward the edge of the fissure and groaned.

"Logan," Kadie moaned. How was he going to get out? The moss-covered walls were sheer. They stood much taller than he, and the crevice was at least seven-feet wide. "Just . . . just wait here. I'll go find a stick . . . something . . . ."

She pushed away from the edge and glanced about frantically, certain there had to be a log or a long stick close by.

"Kadie!" Logan's voice broke through her tumultuous thoughts. "Kadence!" he repeated a bit more impatiently.

Her eyes narrowed, frustrated, and she scrambled back toward the edge and peered down. Their eyes met. "What?" she yelled. Suddenly tears broke through her tough reserve and she sucked in a deep breath. "What?" She sniffed and her voice trembled. Panic threatened to consume her.

"I can't get out of here on my own. By the time you find something to pull me out with, we'll have lost any opportunity to find help. You can't lift me. You need to find that dog. It's getting further away, and we're going to lose our chance. You need to leave me and find help."

"No!" She shook her head. Her tears finally broke free. She brushed at them angrily. "I won't leave you. I won't!"

Her body quaked when a gust of wind tore across her sodden clothes. Logan eyed her. "Kadie," he spoke calmly, but forcefully, "you have to find help."

"That dog is probably some rabid wolf!" she responded, angrily. "It will eat me! I'll get lost! I'll get turned around in the woods and the mist. What if . . . ." A sob tore through her trembling lips. "I can't leave you. What if I can't find you again? I can't, Logan!"

Just then she heard the sound of the animal in the distance. It barked several times. Logan listened then faced her with hard eyes. "Kadie, that is a *dog*—someone's *pet*! You need to go—go now, and get help. Just listen to the dog—follow it. You'll find me again." His tone softened. "I know you will. You can do this," he encouraged. "You need to go, Kadie!"

She inhaled deeply and her eyes narrowed before she pushed away from the edge. Her breathing was shallow and her legs trembled as she worked her way down the boulder. She allowed herself a quick glance back. Her heart pounded against her chest. She felt the rush of blood as it pumped through her veins. How could she do this? How could she leave him? If she lost him . . . She pressed her lips together and focused on the mist-shrouded woods below her, then willed her legs to carry her away from Logan. Her only hope of saving him was to find the dog and its owner as quick as possible. She had to trust she had the strength to save him.

CHAPTER *Thirteen*

*I*t seemed ages before she finally reached the bottom of the ridge and moved into the dark forest. The slippery descent had taxed much of her strength, and her legs felt rubbery and feeble. Her body trembled and her heart beat a frantic rhythm in her ears. Her breathing was ragged as she raced through the dense forest's undergrowth, but she forced her aching feet to carry her quickly over slippery deadfall, moss-covered nurse logs, and tangled patches of ferns.

"Help!" she called as she ran. "Please, help us!"

She listened for the sound of the barking dog, but in the forest it was harder to hear. The yips sounded distorted and smothered by the dense vegetation. She paused and listened. She tried to calm the beating of her heart and listen past the persistent ringing in her ears. The sound came again and she ran frantically toward it, hoping that she wasn't chasing some hungry coyote.

She continued to chase the sound, and her anxiety increased when she drew nearer. "Please don't be a coyote," she muttered as she continued to jog through the trees.

Soon the barking grew louder, and Kadie slowed. She saw a clearing through the trees in the distant and she approached the meadow with cautious steps. The dog's barking grew to a frantic pitch. Kadie spotted the small white-and-black terrier standing on the edge of the meadow. She felt weak with relief.

Catching sight of Kadie, the dog growled and barred its teeth when she approached. "It's okay. It's okay," she tried to calm the dog. "Hello?" Her voice rose as she moved away from the trees.

The dog ran away, growling. It bounded through the tall grass, and Kadie's knees nearly gave way when she spotted a dirty, orange tent standing on the far side of the clearing. A bright, welcoming fire, burned nearby.

"Hello! Hey, hello? I need help!" She rushed across the field. No one answered and Kadie felt confused. She slowed hesitantly. "Hello?" she called.

She approached the tent with some trepidation and watched the dog as it bounded toward a man, kneeling next to the fire.

"Hey, you!" she spoke.

He didn't turn away from the fire or give any indication he'd heard.

She stopped. The man poked a stick in the fire and Kadie eyed him cautiously. He looked young, in his early twenties at most, and his long hair hung in dreadlocks down his bare back. He wore cut-offs and leather sandals. Her eyes narrowed and she moved closer guardedly.

"Sir?" she spoke again when she was only scant feet away. "Sir?" She stepped closer.

His head swiveled around slowly and his eyes suddenly grew large. He jumped to his feet and stumbled backward.

"Watch out!" she yelled when he barely missed stepping into the fire.

"Whoa, man!" he stuttered as he jerked a pair of headphones from his ears. His music player fell into the dirt and he watched Kadie with frightened eyes. "Dude, where'd you come from?"

Kadie's shoulders slumped in relief. She blew out a long, slow breath. "Thank goodness. We need help. We've been lost in these mountains since yesterday. My friend is stuck. He's stuck in a crack in the rocks up on the ridge. We heard your dog," she rushed to explain.

"Are you serious? Man, slow down. This is sick," He looked pale and Kadie wondered if he were going to pass out.

She held her hands out pleading and swallowed hard before she asked, "Can you help us, please?"

"Yeah . . . uh . . . yeah, man. Just, hey, take a breather for a minute." He eyed her warily and Kadie could see the color return to his face.

Her face twisted uncertainly, and the dog licked her hand. She patted the terrier's head absently.

"Brutis—come boy," the man called his dog and stepped over toward his tent. "Hey, I'll . . . uh . . . get some rope, a'right?" He pointed toward the large backpack. "Help yourself to a beer, huh?"

Kadie breathed deeply when the man disappeared into the tent. Her knees felt weak and she hoped they would keep her upright. She inhaled and anxiously gazed at the forest. She closed her eyes, hoping she'd be able to find her way back to Logan and find her way quickly.

"Hang on, Logan," she whispered. Her head shot up when the man exited the tent with a bundle of yellow mooring rope.

"Okay, lead the way." He nodded toward the forest and then called the dog.

The little terrier raced happily ahead of them, barking as it ran through the tall grass. Kadie led the way through the forest as quickly as she could. She wondered if she was going in the right direction. It was difficult not to get turned around in such dense vegetation.

"I'm Kadie Reynolds, by the way," she introduced herself. "Thank you! Thank you for helping us."

"No problem. Name's Mack."

"It's good to meet you." A smile touched her lips while studying his unusual appearance. He remained shirtless, and his cut-off jeans were dirty and ragged. "Have you been camping long? Can you tell me how close we are to a town?"

Mack's eyebrows rose. "Dude, how'd you get lost?"

"Oh, we . . . ," she paused. She wondered how much she should tell him. "We were hiking, and we managed to get turned around."

Her thoughts raced to Logan. Was he still safe? She had been away from him for about an hour or so—or was it longer? She felt disoriented and muddled. *Please help me find Logan,* she voiced silently. Would he be too cold? Would he succumb to hypothermia? Had he been hurt worse than he had let on? She picked up her pace and glanced back toward Mack.

"We heard your dog from up on the ridge," she explained breathlessly. "We were climbing down the ridge when he fell in."

"Wicked! Dude, you were trying to come off that ridge without ropes?" Mack laughed and shook his head. "Man, you're crazy."

Kadie grimaced. "It was faster than turning around. We don't have any gear with us. We needed help, and we were trying to find your dog," she clarified.

"Oh, yeah," he muttered slowly. "Old Brutis was going loopy. I figured he was barking at a squirrel or something."

"Are we close to any towns? Are you backpacking?" she pressed.

"Yeah, I got a truck parked up at Obstruction Point, about five or six miles back. The closest town is Port Angeles, dude," he responded.

Her sudden relief warred with her concern over Logan, but she felt her shoulders relax. They were so close.

* * * * * * *

Logan slumped wearily against the smooth, weather-worn rock. His fingers ached with the strain of trying to climb the vertical wall, and he glanced down at his muddy, bleeding fingers. He felt frustrated and angry. He cursed under his breath and glanced up at the dark clouds overhead. A few stray raindrops fell through the opening in the rocks to land on his head. The cold droplets ran down his hair and dripped onto his neck. He shivered slightly and sat down on the narrow, wet floor of his natural prison.

He laid his head against his arms. How had he managed to get himself into such a mess? He hoped he had not made a mistake sending Kadie on ahead for help. The dog had ceased to bark a while ago, and he hadn't heard a sound other than the wind sighing in the distant trees and the chorus of birds. Had Kadie found someone? Was she lost in the woods? His teeth ground together anxiously as he worried over her.

"Dang it," he muttered, shaking his head.

He shouldn't have sent her on ahead. What if she were hurt, or worse? He glared up at the edge of his hole. He had spent part of his time since Kadie had left trying to climb the slick wall, but his efforts had been useless. The edge was too far up. How would he ever get out of this? He had to get out of the hole, and he could only hope Kadie was not debilitated somewhere in the forest. He wondered if she had found the help they so desperately needed. He had to find Zaza. He knew his daughter was frightened and confused. The thought stole the breath from his lungs and he bit his fist, trying to control his chaotic emotions. *Zaza* . . . . He screamed then laid his head back against the smooth wall and stared, unseeing, toward the dark sky.

He closed his eyes and took several deep breaths. He still couldn't believe his terrible mistake. How had he managed to lose his focus and slip into the fissure? He'd helped Kadie across the wide gap, and just as he'd been about to follow, an unexpected sound from behind had startled him. Confused, he turned quickly and had slipped on the slick moss. His feet had jerked out from underneath him, and he'd toppled over the edge. He cursed his bad sense of judgment and frowned. It could have been worse, he guessed. He could have easily broken a leg, an arm, or his neck.

"Kadie, please be all right," he whispered into the stillness.

He closed his eyes and remembered Kadie's frightened expression. She'd been scared. Her eyes had been filled with fear, but he'd also read a strong determination within their hazel depths. He knew he could trust her to find the help they needed, but this wilderness was a dangerous place. Her image flashed in his mind. Despite the sudden changes in his life since Kadie's appearance, he felt grateful for her presence. He was glad that Kadie was here, and he seemed to take strength in her strength.

She was levelheaded, strong-willed, and a fighter. She had pushed hard through the mountains without complaining even though Logan knew she was bone-tired and her muscles ached. She had even done her best to keep the mood lighter even though she worried for Zaza and Maysha. He knew beyond a doubt that she would continue to stand by him while he fought for his daughter's safe return. He smiled as he remembered Zaza laughing with Kadie only a few nights ago. He felt infinitely grateful that Kadie's fiancé was no longer in the picture.

He had to admit that he had a difficult time trusting women since his divorce. Despite his and Ashley's problems, their divorce and her sudden disappearance from his and Zaza's life had left Logan deeply hurt, and unfortunately many of the women he knew saw only prosperity when they looked his way. He sighed. *That isn't exactly true*, he had to admit.

He'd met many selfish women, who only desired wealth, but

he'd also met many wonderful women—women who had values and integrity—but his heart hadn't been open. He hadn't been willing to see the good qualities in those women. Logan also had to admit his divorce left him jaded where women were concerned. Ashley had hurt him more than he cared to admit. He had attempted to date over the years, but his insecurities always prevented him from seeking a more in-depth relationship with anyone.

Since his divorce with Ashley, he'd been more than a little wary of the opposite sex. Adelaide and Beth had encouraged him to remarry, but he had yet to find a woman who appealed to him on the level that Kadence Reynolds did. Kadie was different. He'd sensed that almost immediately. He knew that she didn't see just Logan Matthews, the lawyer, or Logan Matthews, the bachelor. She saw *him*, and he felt comfortable with that. She also awakened feeling in him that had been dormant for years. He sighed and rubbed the back of his neck.

His thoughts centered once again on Zaza. His daughter didn't usually take to strangers so quickly. She was a bright, energetic little girl, but she was often very introverted and shy. He closed his eyes and his breath caught in his throat. The thought of his smiling little girl caused a strangled sound to burst from his lips. She would be frightened and scared. Were they taking care of her? Was she alone? The thought clawed at his heart, and he felt as if he would bleed internally. He leaned his head into his hands. They had to get out of here. He had to get his little girl back! He had to trust that Kadie would return soon. She was his only hope.

* * * * * * *

"Logan!" Kadie hollered when they neared the craggy fissure.

Her breathing was ragged as she climbed the rocky ridge. The sound of Mack's labored breathing sounded behind her, and the terrier bounded ahead. She cringed when the little dog teetered precariously close to an edge and Mack whistled for the dog. The little dog loped past her and licked her hand as it trotted toward Mack.

"Logan!" she called again.

"Kadie?" she heard an answering call, and relief made her knees weak.

"We're coming. Hang on," she returned. She pushed her legs to climb the slippery boulders. She glanced back toward Mack. "He's here! Hurry, bring the rope."

"Coming, lady, coming," he panted, and the terrier yipped happily.

Kadie reached the edge and peered over the side down toward Logan. Their eyes met, and she could read the plethora of emotions in his gaze. He smiled, and his shoulders fell with relief. He laughed.

"You did it," he whispered. "I knew you could."

"I found help!" she assured him. She turned and watched as Mack approached the edge. "He's here." She pointed down toward Logan, and Mack moved closer to peer into the yawning gap.

"Hey, man. Hold on, alright?" Mack told him.

He moved back down the ridge a few feet and began working the rope around another boulder. The dog raced to the edge of the fissure and barked at Logan.

"Brutis, cool it boy," Mack called.

Kadie moved back to the edge and patted the little dog absently while she kept her eyes on Logan's. Her relief was overwhelming, and she smiled into his dark eyes. She had been so afraid she wouldn't find her way back to him.

"Thank you, Kadie," Logan murmured, staring up toward her.

The little dog growled when he spoke, and Kadie grinned. Brutis licked Kadie and then barked again.

"And thank you, too." Logan nodded toward the little dog.

"He's as ferocious as a wolf." She scratched Brutis' ears.

"Hey, lady, come and hold on to this rope in case this loop gives," Mack called.

Startled, her eyes widened, and she pushed away from the ridge, holding fast to the rope while Mack assisted Logan from the hole. Her heart picked up pace when she watched Logan's head appear over the edge, and he rolled his long body onto the flat surface of the boulder. He stood slowly, and their eyes met before Logan turned his attention to Mack.

"Thank you." He stepped toward Mack and shook his hand firmly. "You don't know how nice it is to see you. I appreciate the help."

"No problem," Mack returned lazily and then nudged Brutis with his foot when he continued to bark at Logan.

Logan tried to pat the little dog, but Brutis snapped and ran back toward Kadie, barring his teeth. Relieved, she released the rope and patted Brutis when he nudged her leg with his wet nose.

"I see you made a loyal friend." Logan stepped toward her with a smile.

She brushed past the dog and stepped toward Logan, then fell into his arms with a relieved sigh. He held her tightly against him, and he buried his face in her tangled, wet hair. His hot breath brushed against her neck, and she pushed her face against his chest as she spoke his name.

"Logan," she breathed.

His arms tightened around her. He kissed her forehead. "I'm glad you were safe."

He pulled back and kissed her lips. His kiss was brief and tender, and she inhaled sharply when he pulled away. Her body trembled with varied emotions, and she glanced down at her feet when he turned away to speak with Mack once more.

"How far are we from the nearest town?"

"Closest town is Port Angeles, man," Mack returned. Logan's brows creased thoughtfully, and Mack continued, "Yeah, dude, listen—I've got a truck parked at Obstruction Point. It's about six miles or so from my camp, man. I can give you two a lift into town," he offered.

Kadie smiled her relief.

Logan nodded. "I'd appreciate that."

"Thank you, Mack," Kadie added.

They followed Mack down the ridge and into the forest. It didn't take them long to reach Mack's camp and Kadie felt exceptionally relieved to see the man's tent on the edge of the woods. They'd finally be out of the wilderness. Kadie knew Logan wanted to waste no time finding Senator Jukes, and she desperately hoped they would find Zaza safe. What had happened since she and Logan had been in the mountains?

She grasped her nervous stomach when they entered Mack's campsite. He threw the rope into the tent and then rummaged through his backpack. He pulled out a few apples and a couple of granola bars. He tossed them to Logan before he pulled a six pack of beer from inside the pack and raised it high.

"Beer?" he asked nonchalantly.

Logan accepted the apples and granola bars, but declined the beer graciously. "No, thanks, but I appreciate the food. Do you have any water?" he replied.

Mack opened a can of beer and took a generous gulp. He wiped his mouth and tossed his dreadlocks back from off his shoulder. "Naw, but I have a filter and there's a stream down that way, dude," he replied before he belched loudly.

Kadie chuckled, and Logan's mouth twisted in amusement. "We'll gladly compensate you for all your trouble."

Mack grinned. "No way, man. Like I said, it's no problem. Come on—truck's this way. Brutis, come." He whistled loudly and turned to lead the way.

After visiting the small stream for a drink of water, Logan and Kadie ate their apples and granola bars as they followed Mack through dense forest. Brutis trotted next to Kadie. She patted his head intermittently and tossed him small crumbs from her granola bar. He licked her hand and then peered at Logan with a snarl.

"Looks like I have competition," Logan murmured.

Kadie blushed and suppressed a small smile as they left the forest behind them and entered a subalpine meadow. Their breathing grew more ragged when they climbed higher, and soon they were on a steep ridge, overlooking another vast, open meadow. Wildflowers grew abundantly and swayed in the gentle breeze. Kadie could smell their unique, spicy perfume. The meadow was beautiful.

Mack continued to lead the way along the ridge, and the three remained silent. The sounds of the forest surrounded them, and she felt grateful Mack didn't bombard them with questions. It would be difficult to explain the immensity of their problem. Soon, they left the ridge and followed a well-worn dirt path through the thick trees, and Kadie felt ever-more grateful. The path made walking much easier. The last two days had been difficult trying to cross such varied vegetation, and a man-made trail also meant they were nearing their destination.

Her body relaxed, and Logan squeezed her hand. The dog barked and bounded on ahead with Mack, and Logan took the opportunity to ask, "What did you tell him?"

"I told him we were turned around while hiking." She shrugged.

He nodded thoughtfully. "Good."

The sun was beginning to set in the sky, and dark clouds hung on the horizon when they finally reached Mack's red Toyota Tacoma. His vehicle was covered in layers of dried mud. Beer cans littered the interior, and Mack brushed the cans to the floor with a flourish.

"Get in," he ordered as he jumped behind the wheel.

Brutis jumped into the cab of the truck and Kadie slid in beside him. Her nose twitched slightly as the sour scent of stale beer, and the sickly, sweet smell of marijuana assaulted her. Logan squeezed in next to Kadie and slammed the door while Mack turned the key. The little engine sputtered and died. He swore loudly and turned the key again. Kadie held her breath as she listened to the engine gasp. *Please start*, she voiced anxiously.

"Come on you piece of . . . aha!" He crowed when the engine finally turned and growled to life. "I've been having trouble with the carburetor."

Kadie sighed and relaxed against the seat. She was fond of Mack, despite his unusual character. She was grateful for his laid-back personality and his willingness to help. She didn't know where they'd be had he not been so willing to lend a hand. It felt wonderful to be out of the wilderness and on their way back to civilization and their family. Her relief, however, was marred with worry. Her anxiety over Maysha and Zaza increased. How would they find Zaza? And were Maysha, Beth, and Adelaide all right? Had they been harmed? Unanswered questions made her stomach turn uncomfortably.

"Where did you say you guys were coming from again?" Mack's voice suddenly cut into her turbulent thoughts. "Because, dude, you guys were way off the trail." He laughed.

Logan smiled. "We were coming from Moose Lake."

"Yeah? Wow, hey, did you get in a fist fight or something? Where'd you get the awesome shiner, dude?" Mack grinned.

Kadie glanced at Logan's bruised eye. She'd forgotten about that.

"Yes," Logan replied matter-of-factly. "I did. I let an argument get out of hand."

"Hey, cool, man. I understand that."

Isn't that an understatement, she mused humorlessly. Kadie bit her bottom lip. She hoped he would not ask any more questions, and she breathed a sigh of relief when Mack reached for the truck's radio.

"Hey, you like rock?" Mack asked and cranked the volume, filling the little cab with heavy metal music.

She caught Logan's eye and he wrapped an arm around her shoulder. "Try to rest," he murmured against her ear.

His hot breath sent pleasant shivers down her spine. She laid her head against his shoulder and willed her weary body to relax against his. She stared out of the darkened window as they passed the ranger station on the border of the park, and Mack drove his truck into a populated section of town. Lights shone from many of the homes lining the streets, and they passed several cars.

She watched the houses go by in a blur, and she suddenly craved the comforts of home. It felt as if she had spent ages away from society, even though she and Logan had been lost for only a couple of days. She closed her eyes. Mack sang loudly with the music, and Kadie's stomach clenched again as she thought of Zaza and Maysha.

* * * * * *

Mack pulled the truck into the parking lot of a brightly-lit grocery store, and Kadie suddenly wondered what they would do now that they had reached town. Would Logan go straight to the police? They had no money, no phone, and no transportation. How far was Port Angeles from Bremerton? She looked to Logan and watched silently as his jaw tightened and relaxed.

Mack flipped the radio off, and the silence in the little cab seemed almost deafening. Brutis jumped onto her lap and licked her face. Kadie laughed tersely and pushed the little dog down.

"Do you have a phone we can borrow?" she asked.

Mack shrugged. "Yeah, sure."

Logan's eyes met hers when Mack reached past Kadie and opened the truck's glove compartment. Old hamburger wrappers and empty cigarette sleeves spilled out onto Logan's lap as Mack rummaged inside for his cell phone.

"Here, man. Not sure how much juice it still has." He tossed the phone to Kadie, and she passed it on to Logan.

Logan grasped the phone with a curt smile. "Thanks," he spoke and he stepped from the vehicle.

Kadie was quick to follow, and Brutis leaped from the cab of the truck. The terrier jumped at her legs, and she bent to pat his head as Logan held the phone to his ear. She waited with bated breath while the phones connected.

"Beth!"

Kadie's eyes shot to his.

"Beth . . . yes," Logan went on. "We're all right. I'll explain later. Yes—she's fine, just very tired. Listen, I don't have time to explain. We're in Port Angeles, just off of Lincoln Street. Are you in a position to come and get us?"

Kadie listened intently, and it was a long moment before he spoke again, "Yes—thank you. We'll wait here. Be careful, Beth. Goodbye."

He shut the phone.

"They're all right?" she whispered.

He nodded. The relief was evident in his expression. "Yes, she'll be here as soon as she can." He touched her shoulder gently as he walked past her and moved toward Mack's truck.

He returned the phone, and Kadie joined him.

"Hey, Brutis, get in the cab, man," Mack called the dog, and Kadie rubbed the little terrier's head once more before it jumped into the littered cab. An empty beer can fell out onto the pavement with a loud clatter, and she watched as it rolled under the truck. Brutis barked, demanding her attention.

The little dog's tongue lolled as she tugged its ear. She hugged Brutis tightly, and he snapped at Logan with a vicious snarl when he tried to pet him. Kadie laughed a little, and Logan scowled. "Thanks anyway, Brutis," he told the dog and took a moment to shake Mack's hand. "I appreciate all of your help. I don't know what we would have done without you."

Mack shrugged. "Hey, no problem. Good luck, man. You and

your girl have a cool night." Logan nodded before he shut the cab door.

Kadie raised her hand in a farewell gesture as Mack peeled the tires of the truck, and he raced out of the parking lot. She spun to face Logan. The streetlamps cast mottled shadows across his dark face, and he turned to meet her gaze.

"What's going on? Did Beth tell you anything?"

He ran a hand across his bearded face and grimaced. "They're all fine, but worried. I guess our friend the Senator has been in touch with them as well," he responded before his eyes scanned the parking lot. "Let's go sit down and wait. It will be nearly an hour before Beth gets here."

Logan grasped her elbow gently. He led her from beneath the bright lights and toward a metal bench near the darkened street.

"Zaza? Do they know anything? Anything more about Zaza?" she asked tersely.

Logan sat down on the bench and she slumped next to him. His body heat radiated through his thin shirt, warming her, and she resisted the urge to lean in against him.

He shook his head. "No," he answered. Kadie exhaled. "They haven't heard anything more since the night they dumped us in the mountains. She didn't have a lot of time to tell me much more." He replied. "We'll find out more when she gets here."

Kadie reached out instinctively and touched his forearm. "Kadie," he whispered her name and covered her hand with his before he wrapped an arm around her shoulder. He pressed a kiss against her forehead, and she leaned in, seeking comfort in his touch. "What now, Logan?" She swallowed hard.

She felt his body tense. "We find Senator Jukes," he replied brusquely.

CHAPTER *Fourteen*

$\mathcal{K}$ adie opened her weary eyes as a loud squeal sounded nearby. She felt Logan tense, and she bolted upright when a vehicle screeched to a stop next to the curb. The car's door flew open, and she breathed her relief when Beth nearly fell out of the vehicle.

"Logan—Kadie?" Logan's sister called frantically as she righted herself and then flew toward them. She caught Logan around the neck. "You're okay. I've been so worried. We haven't heard anything in days. We thought . . . ." Her voice cracked on a sob as he grasped her upper arms and pulled her gently from him.

"I'm fine, Beth," he reassured his sister.

He kissed her cheek before she caught sight of his bruised face in the fluorescent lights, and she moaned, "Oh, look what those thugs did to you."

Logan grimaced. "Really, it's fine. I'm glad to see you."

Beth glanced at Kadie and she gasped quietly. "Kadie!" She threw her arms around Kadie and squeezed. "Maysha has gone crazy with worry. She stayed back to watch Adelaide. She is so relieved. We've been out of our minds worrying, and Adelaide . . . ," she paused, and her lips trembled.

Logan's brows knit together. "How is she?"

"I think she's taken a turn for the worse, Logan," Beth murmured. "We've kept what was going on from her the best we could, but she's slipping. I don't think she understands a whole lot anyway. And . . . Zaza!" A sob tore through Beth's lips.

Logan's shoulders slumped wearily. He ran a hand through his hair. "Beth," he spoke gruffly. "We need to get into Seattle. I need to find that monster who took Zaza and get some answers."

Kadie caught Logan's eye and she turned to Beth with a worried frown. "He took Zaza," she whispered.

Beth swallowed hard and nodded. "I know. Get in. I'll tell you everything I know."

A tear rolled down Beth's cheek, and she brushed at it with an agitated hand while she turned for the car. They rushed to get in.

"Tell me what happened. Everything, Beth," Logan spoke while they drove through Port Angeles.

Kadie stared out the darkened window and watched as the lights of the town screamed by. Beth pushed the little car to a neck-breaking speed, and her knuckles showed white on the steering wheel as she struggled to explain.

"It was early in the morning. I thought . . . well, I thought Kadie had decided to come back to the house, so I didn't hesitate to answer the door. A man with a hood over his face forced his way into the house. I screamed. He told me he had a message and that if I ever wanted to see you and Zaza again, I needed to listen and do what the letter instructed.

"My scream must have awakened Maysha, because she came downstairs. It didn't take her long to realize what was going on. She tried to get away—to go for help, but the man caught her. He slapped her. She attacked him, but he pulled a gun and repeated what he had told me. He said they had Kadie too—he told us if we talked, you would be killed immediately. He said to stay put and wait, and they would be in touch."

"What did the letter say?" Logan's expression hardened.

Beth pulled a wrinkled letter from her jacket pocket and handed it Logan. Her lips pressed together, and Kadie watched with bated breath as Logan unfolded its creases and opened the letter with trembling hands. With a deep breath, he began to read aloud.

"'You and your family are being watched at all times. If you go to the police, we will not hesitate to take action. You will wait for our call in a few days' time to give you further instructions. If your brother returns, he is to call this number, and he will then be given instructions to coordinate the safe return of his daughter.'" Logan read the number scrawled across the bottom of the note. His teeth ground together. "*If I return?*" He crumpled the note in his fist.

"Give me your phone, Beth," he instructed. Despite his anger, his voice sounded amazingly calm.

Beth passed him her cell phone, and Kadie waited anxiously as he placed the receiver to his ear. Several moments passed in silence. When no one answered, he punched in the number again. Again, there was no answer, and he shook his head, frustrated.

"Logan?" Kadie asked.

"There's no answer," he spoke between tightly clenched teeth.

"What do you want to do?" Beth asked quietly.

"I want to go Seattle. I'm going to find Senator Jukes," he responded. He tossed the crumpled letter onto the vehicle's floor.

Beth looked his way. "Is that the wisest thing to do?"

He nodded, and they all jumped when the little phone rang. Logan fumbled with the small phone for a brief second and then flipped it open.

"Hello?"

Kadie's brow furrowed, and she listened with bated breath. Logan's shoulders slumped, and Kadie's eyes narrowed when she recognized the shrill chatter coming from the small phone.

"We're all right . . . yes, Maysha. Calm down, she's right here," he spoke into the phone before he handed it back to Kadie with an expressionless face.

Kadie placed the phone to her ear, trying to hold back tears. "Maysha?"

"Where have you been? Did they hurt you? Kadie—I've been so worried. Why did you ever find that *stupid* can? " Maysha cried frantically.

Kadie suppressed a tearful laugh. It had never been so good to hear her sister's angry chatter, and she hugged the phone to her ear. "I'm all right. Really—it's okay; just calm down. Are you okay?"

"No! No, I'm not *okay*. I've been sick, worrying over you!" Maysha yelled.

"I'm safe, honestly. Listen, I can't talk now, but I'm fine. Just . . . just stay in the house and don't answer the door, alright?"

Would Maysha be safe now that Beth had left the house? Would Senator Jukes' men go after her sister? The thought caused a cold sweat to break out across her body.

"Maysha," Kadie spoke again. "Did you hear me?"

"Aren't you coming? Where are you?"

"We are coming. We are—but just not yet. We have to go to Seattle first. We have to find Senator Jukes and—"

"*Seattle?*" Maysha screeched. "Kadie! You get back here *now!*"

Kadie cringed, and she rushed to explain, "Calm down, please. They still have Zaza. We have to find Senator Jukes—we have to get Zaza back." Her sister remained silent for so long she wondered if the connection had dropped. She pulled the phone from her ear. "Maysha?" she asked. She could hear her sister's soft, quiet sobs. Kadie closed her eyes and forced back her own tears. "Maysha?"

"Kadie, *please*—I'm so scared. I'm so worried. What if . . . ?" Maysha sobbed in earnest.

Her own emotions suddenly spilled over, and she hugged the phone tightly. "It'll be okay, it has to be. I promise. We'll come home soon—as soon as we can. We have to find Zaza."

Her sister sniffed loudly. "I know. I love you, Kadie," she croaked.

"I love you too. We'll be there as soon as we can. Please be careful. Please? I have to go now."

Maysha sniffed again. The sound echoed in Kadie's ear. "Knock that old jerk out of this world for me! If I ever get my hands on him, I'll make him wish his mama had been barren!"

Kadie cringed. "Listen, don't do anything crazy. Be careful. We'll be there as soon as we can."

"Hurry back," Maysha whispered, and Kadie closed her eyes when the connection ended.

Silently, she handed the phone back to Logan. She sniffed and wiped her damp tears with the back of her hand. Logan turned to face her. He reached for her hand, and she gratefully placed her fingers in his.

"Kadie, this isn't your fight, you know. I can take you back. You and Maysha don't have to be a part of this any longer."

Her eyes grew large. She felt stunned. The thought had not even crossed her mind. She could not—*would* not—leave Logan now. Her head shot up. "No!" she spoke. "No, I can't! I can't leave now. I'm staying with you!"

Logan's eyes brightened only a little, and he squeezed her hand tightly. He brought her fingers to his lips and brushed them across his mouth. "We still have a while before we reach Seattle. Try to sleep some, huh? I'll wake you before we get there."

* * * * * * *

"Kadie—Kadie, wake up."

Kadie's eyes fluttered open, and she felt momentarily disoriented. Her body slumped at an uncomfortable angle, and her neck ached. She sat up, forcing back a moan, and rubbed her sore muscles as her eyes met Logan's. He squeezed her shoulder gently.

"We're nearly there," he murmured before he turned to face the front.

She yawned and glanced out the window at the bright lights of Seattle. The kaleidoscope of color flooded the little car. She must have slipped into a deep sleep just after leaving Port Angeles. She was surprised they were already in the city. It had seemed only moments since she had closed her eyes.

She brought a hand to her twisting stomach and watched Logan silently. She knew he was nervous. His face was drawn. His eyes were angry and tense. The strong muscles in his jaw convulsed as Beth drove the vehicle through the busy streets of the city. Beth remained silent and her eyes were agonized.

Kadie turned to stare out the window once again, and she focused on breathing deeply when they left the inner-city lights behind and entered the semi-familiar neighborhood where Senator Jukes lived. The immaculate homes stood like sentinels as they drove up the hill, and Kadie stared out the window warily.

"This is it." Logan pointed ahead.

"Are you sure about this? Shouldn't we contact the police first?" Beth asked, her voice trembling.

"No—you two wait here," he instructed, his voice edged with anger.

Without hesitation, he bolted from the car, and Kadie scrambled to follow. She heard Beth exit the vehicle and her hurried steps followed Kadie's.

Logan turned with a scowl. "No, Kadie—Beth. Stay in the car."

Kadie laughed humorlessly. "Absolutely not. You aren't going in that house alone."

"Right," Beth replied. "Come on." She stepped past Logan and advanced up the walk.

His sister stepped up onto the porch and knocked soundly. Kadie rushed to join her, and Logan followed with a scowl. The three waited impatiently, and after moments had passed, Logan pounded loudly against the wood. Kadie rang the doorbell, and she tensed when she heard the unmistakable sound of footsteps drawing near. The door swung open, and bright light spilled across the porch.

Lillian Jukes stood rigid, framed in the immense doorway. "Yes?" she asked curtly. A frown marred her face.

"I need to speak with the Senator immediately." Logan's voice betrayed his anger.

The woman's eyes filled with anxiety, and her hands fluttered nervously. "He isn't here," she returned. "Come back later."

She moved to shut the door, but Logan's hand shot out, and he forced his body partially into the house.

"Where is he?" he demanded.

The older woman raised a trembling hand to the base of her throat. She watched Logan cautiously.

"He . . . he's had a stroke. My husband and he are at Northwest Hospital downtown. There's nothing I can do to help you," she replied with a quaking voice.

"Where is my daughter?" Logan asked through clenched teeth.

Lillian's mouth trembled and tears clouded her vision. Her face turned a sickly, ashen white. Kadie took a tentative step toward her, worried that the older woman was about to faint. Lillian grasped the door, and her knuckles stood out white against the dark wood.

"I . . . I can't help you—I don't know. Please leave, or I'll be forced to call the police," she whispered.

Logan laughed. He sounded slightly crazed, and Kadie regarded him with wary eyes. She touched his arm in an attempt to calm him.

"*Call the police?*" he asked, his voice incredulous.

Lillian swallowed hard and she sniffed. "He's at Northwest. Please . . . please leave." A frightened sob shook her body. "My husband is at Northwest. You need to speak with him."

With a groan, Logan moved his hand away from the door. He stood back abruptly, and they watched with frustration when Lillian slammed the door. Logan's breathing was hard and fast, and his fists clenched into balls. Kadie instinctively reached toward him. He caught her hand in a quick, crushing grip. His eyes closed. His nostrils flared.

"Logan?" she pressed tentatively.

His eyes flew open and he looked directly into Kadie's gaze. He brought her hand to his mouth and then whispered roughly, "Let's go."

* * * * * * *

Beth pulled the car into a slot in the brightly-lit parking lot of Northwest Hospital. Low clouds hung in the sky and soft rain fell onto the parked cars. Raindrops glistened in the light from the overhead lamps and ran in shimmering rivulets down the car's windows. The hospital was busy. Groups of people walked in and out of the immense glass doors. Cars lined up around the front entrance as relatives loaded patients in their vehicles, and nurses wheeled patients to and from the cars. An ambulance drove through the parking lot and turned toward the emergency loading dock. Its flashing lights cast mottled shadows, and strange patterns danced across the crowded lot. They exited the vehicle.

The glass doors slid open at their arrival, and Kadie took in her surroundings with curious eyes. Elaborate window displays lined the wide hall, leading to the impressive front desk.

Logan approached the desk self-assuredly and asked in a businesslike manner, "Adam Jukes please."

The tiny, white-haired secretary's eyes widened at their unusual, sordid appearance and she asked, "Are you a relative?"

"No, I'm an attorney—Logan Matthews. I have business with the Senator and his son, Kenny Jukes," he replied gruffly.

Beth rushed forward to place a square business card on the desk. With parted lips, the older woman tore her eyes away and skimmed the card. "He's . . . well . . . sir . . . ?" She glanced again at his and Kadie's unusual appearance, and he groaned.

"Look, I know we're a mess, but I don't have time to explain. This is important. I need to speak with him immediately," Logan cut in.

The lady shook her head, bewildered, and shrugged. "He . . . he's in room 324, Mr. Matthews. Top level and to your left."

"Thank you," he replied, and without waiting for a response, he pushed away from the desk and turned toward the elevators.

Kadie's stomach knotted when they boarded the over-sized elevator. Several patients and family members crowded in behind them. She tried to ignore the curious stares as everyone noticed their battered appearance, and she held her breath as the elevator climbed to the top floor. Without a word, Logan reached to grasp her hand in his. His face remained stoic. Kadie could tell he was angry and tense. She heard Beth sigh quietly, and she turned to face Logan's sister. Their eyes locked, and she leaned her head against Kadie's shoulder for a brief moment.

Kadie reached out and patted Beth's back as the elevator finally reached the top level. The crowd of people exited the elevator and moved down the hallway while Logan stalled momentarily. He waited for the crowd to disperse before he turned left. He kept Kadie's hand in his. His balmy hand clung to hers, and she hoped Logan had the strength necessary to face Senator Jukes and remain calm.

They soon reached the end of the hall where it branched two ways. Logan skimmed the directory before he turned right, in the direction of Senator Jukes' room. They crossed through an immaculate waiting area that smelled of freshly brewed coffee and Kadie's stomach growled when they passed a table full of complimentary donuts and scones. She grasped her rumbling stomach with her free hand. The small snack they had eaten during their hike with Mack seemed ages ago. She groaned and forced her thoughts to Senator Jukes.

If the Senator had suffered a stroke, then what had become of Zaza? She closed her eyes momentarily and clutched Logan's hand when they drew near the nurses' station.

Suddenly Logan looked down and whispered, "I'm glad you're here."

"Me too," she returned sincerely.

He didn't pause at the nurse's station and when they rushed past, a young nurse, wearing bright pink scrubs, stood and called, "You aren't permitted past this point, sir."

Kadie glanced back, but Logan tugged her hand, and she and Beth followed him in silence. The nurse ran around the station and stepped into the hall.

"Sir," she called. Her voice carried down the corridor. "Sir, you aren't allowed past this point."

He ignored the woman's protests and continued toward the room. Kadie's hand trembled as they neared the door.

"Sir!" the nurse repeated, hurrying down the hall.

Without a glance back, Logan released her hand and burst through the door. The wood door slammed against the door stop with a loud thump. Kadie hesitated in the doorway as he stormed into the extensive hospital room, and she watched with wide eyes as Kenny Jukes nearly fell out of his chair with surprise.

Kenny swore loudly. Righting himself, he bolted to his feet.

Logan's fists balled at his side and he glared at Kenny, his eyes filled with rage, while the Senator remained deathly still in his hospital bed. Kadie could hear the sound of an oxygen machine and the soft beeping of a heart monitor. She stepped cautiously into the room and her eyes focused on Senator Jukes. His eyes remained closed. Tubes ran from his nose and mouth. Monitors clung to his bare chest, and his ribs rose and fell weakly.

"Hey!" The nurse entered the room.

Kadie pulled her eyes away from the Senator and faced the young woman with wary eyes. The nurse's breathing was ragged, and she was visibly trembling. Her brown eyes widened when she took in the scene before her. Logan stood stone-still, his eyes focused intently on Kenny Jukes, who looked as though he had seen a ghost. Kenny's face was pale and drawn, and Kadie detected a slight quiver of his hands.

"Where is my daughter?" Logan asked slowly. Rage caused his voice to tremble.

Beth stood in the door frame, her eyes reflected her fear.

"You people aren't allowed in here. You need to leave immediately," the nurse spoke firmly and she grasped Logan's shoulder.

Logan shrugged the nurse's hand off his arm and he spoke again, "Where is my daughter?"

Kenny Jukes stood straight. His eyes traveled across the group. "I don't know what you mean," he replied stiffly.

Suddenly, Logan shot across the room and Beth let out a startled gasp when he caught Kenny Jukes by the collar of his expensive white shirt. He slammed the man against the wall. Logan trembled with rage, and Kenny coward in fear.

"I'm calling security," the nurse yelled.

Senator Jukes still lay motionless in the bed and Kadie swallowed hard. Her eyes shot back toward Logan and Kenny.

Logan shook the older man. He screamed in his face, "I said 'where is my daughter'? Where is she?"

"Get your hands off of me!" Kenny demanded, twisting out of Logan's grasp.

"Sir, I've called security. They'll be here any moment. You people need to leave immediately." The nurse's voice trembled and she glared at Kadie and Beth.

"Not until I get an answer," Logan stepped back, but blocked the man's path.

Kenny stood still and he glared at Logan. "And just how do you think you're going to help your daughter when you're in jail?"

Logan's jaw clenched. He took another menacing step toward Kenny, and the man's eyes popped wide. He stumbled slightly just as two armed officers stepped into the room. Kadie's heart constricted and she swallowed hard, eyeing the officers warily.

"Is there a problem here?" the beefier of the two asked.

Logan didn't remove his eyes from Kenny, but Kenny shook his head calmly.

"No, officer," he spoke coolly. "Mr. Matthews and his friends were just leaving. We had a bit of a misunderstanding." Kenny eyed Logan meaningfully. "I suggest you go *home*, Mr. Matthews. Or I will have you arrested. It won't do anyone any good if you're in jail."

"Sir?" the officer stepped toward Logan. "Do I need to take you into custody?"

Logan stepped back, and his eyes fell on Adam Jukes, lying in the bed. The oxygen concentrator continued to wheeze, and Kadie watched Logan.

"Logan," she spoke, and his eyes shot to hers. She licked her dry lips and nodded. Her eyes shot to Kenny Jukes' warily. "We should leave."

"Yes, please. I will be in touch, Mr. Matthews." Kenny added and turned away to face the window.

Logan's nostrils flared, and he stepped toward Kenny Jukes.

"Logan!" Beth called warningly, and he paused.

His shoulders fell, and he took a deep breath. He spun around and eyed the officers with disdain before his angry gaze swung back and locked on Kenny Jukes' back.

"I had better hear from you—*soon*," he spoke between tightly clenched teeth.

"Come on," Kadie grasped his arm and tugged him toward the door.

His body remained tense as they left the room, and Kadie exhaled as the officers escorted them down the hall in silence. People glanced curiously at the small group, and Kadie knew she and Logan were a mess. They were both wet and dirty, and her hair felt plastered to her skull. She silently wondered what people were thinking as they retraced their steps through the hospital. They exited the building and stepped into the drizzling rain. The officers turned to face Logan.

"I don't want to see you near here. Any more problems and I'll arrest you on the spot. Do you understand, Mr. Matthews?" The beefy officer's eyes traveled meaningfully across the three, and he paused, noting Logan and Kadie's appearance. "What happened to you two? He asked gruffly.

Logan's eyes narrowed. "We were hiking." His voice held a hard edge.

The officer's brow rose. "You expect me to believe that?"

"Believe whatever you want," Logan returned. "What I do and how we look is our business."

"Just get out of here," the officer returned before he stepped back through the automatic doors and disappeared.

Tears ran in rivulets down Beth's cheeks, and she began sobbing quietly. Logan moaned, and Kadie grasped his hand, forcing back tears of her own. Where was Zaza? Her own frustrations felt as if they would drown her. She glanced at Logan anxiously. She couldn't begin to imagine what depth of agony he was experiencing.

He took several deep breaths before he spoke, "Let's go back to the car. We'll return to his place in a few hours."

They walked toward their vehicle. Kadie was beyond frustrated, but she remained silent.

Beth slipped behind the steering wheel, and she looked to Logan desperately. "What are we going to do? We need help," she spoke between sobs.

Logan's face was pale and drawn. He leaned his head back against the headrest. He remained silent for several tense moments, and Kadie watched as his brows creased in thought. "We're going to get some answers, but right now, we need to think logically. Kadie and I need to get some food in our systems. We haven't had much to eat, and we're dehydrated. We've spent too many hours hiking. We'll get something to eat and drink, clean up a little, and head back to his place. We'll wait as long as necessary, but we are going to get some answers—tonight!"

Beth nodded, and Kadie swallowed hard as she slumped back against the backseat. She let her aching head fall wearily against the headrest. Her stomach turned, and she wondered if she would be able to hold any food down when Beth pulled the car back onto the busy street.

"Beth," Logan suddenly murmured. "Pull over—you can't drive like this."

Beth wiped at her damp cheeks and shook her head.

"Let me drive," he pressed.

"You can't drive," she responded with a garbled sob.

"Beth, if I don't do something—I'm going to go insane. I'll be fine—you're weaving across lanes, sis."

She sniffed and pulled the vehicle to the curb. They sat in silence for a moment before Logan moved to exit. He opened the passenger door just as the cell phone rang. Kadie jumped instinctively, and Logan scrambled to answer the phone.

Kadie held her breath.

"Matthews here!" Logan spoke.

His body stiffened. He listened for several tense moments, and Beth watched him with wide, fearful eyes. She and Kadie shared a worried look, and Kadie felt her nails digging into her soft palm. She forced herself to relax. Who was calling? What was happening?

"All right," Logan spoke again. A moment later he shut the phone.

"Who was it?" Kadie asked, her voice trembling.

He turned in his seat to include both Beth and Kadie. "That was Kenny Jukes. He wants to meet at a café along the pier in an hour."

At least that was something. It was something they could grasp and hang onto. Maybe then they would get the answers they were seeking. Maybe they would get Zaza. She shut her eyes. *Please let this be our answer.*

"Is that wise? What if . . . ," Beth asked, her voice weak.

He shook his head and answered abruptly, "He can't do anything to us. The café is too public. Remember he has an *illustrious name* to protect. Isn't that what this is all about?"

Beth ducked her head in frustration. "Where is the café?" she asked.

"It's about two blocks from my office, but I've been thinking—I want to stop at the office. I have some small recording devices—"

"Won't that look suspicious, Logan? It's nearly midnight. We can't go to your office," Beth interjected.

"No, it won't look suspicious. I've gone in to work cases late before and the building is empty this time of night. Besides, we need to clean up and get a bit more to eat. I have an extra suit and a few essentials at the office, and—" His eyes strayed to Kadie's.

"I have a shirt and a jacket in the trunk that will fit Kadie," Beth jumped in. "But the pants . . . ." She frowned, and Kadie smiled wanly.

"Fine. Now listen, after we've cleaned up, we'll strap on the recording devices. I want each one of us to wear one. They are small and not likely to be detected without a full body search. Senator Jukes is not going to do this to my family and get away with it! I'll see them all rot in prison before this over!"

CHAPTER *Fifteen*

Logan's teeth ground together as he stepped into the darkened café. Kadie and Beth followed close behind, and he was once again infinitely grateful for Kadie's presence. He forced his body to relax a fraction. It wouldn't do his daughter any good if he broke Kenny Jukes' nose before he had the chance to tell Logan where to find her. He closed his eyes and hoped this would soon be over, and he would have Zaza in his arms once more.

He'd never spent any significant time away from her, and he knew his daughter would be frightened. The thought made his blood boil, and he focused on taking deep, calming breaths. He clenched his fists together as he weaved through the crowded tables of the café, searching for Kenny. He caught sight of the older man, sitting in the back corner of the café, away from the other late-night diners.

He felt Kadie's hand reach for his, and instinctively he wrapped her hand in his. Her fingers trembled, and he knew both she and Beth were nervous and frightened. He was surprised how well Beth was holding up under the nerve-racking circumstances, and Kadie's resiliency left him in awe, especially considering all she had endured over the past few days.

He knew Kadie's strength had been taxed with their treacherous hike in the mountains, and they had both had very little to eat. The small amount they'd been able to harvest in the woods hadn't been nearly enough to keep up their strength, and even with the small snacks they'd eaten since their rescue, he knew her strength was waning. He owed her a lot for standing by him. After all, hadn't he gotten them in this mess? He'd known from the moment he'd mentioned the family's old connection, he was stirring the hornets' nest.

Logan had deliberately provoked Adam Jukes, but he had no idea what lengths the senator would take to protect his secret. What had happened to Charlotte and the Clarke family? Logan closed his eyes, and his jaw convulsed. Had his daughter suffered the same fate? *No*, his mind screamed.

Determined to find answers, he turned in the direction of Kenny Jukes' obscure table. Kenny greeted them with a stiff nod, and Logan glowered as he sat in the chair opposite him. Kadie sat next to Logan, and Beth pulled a chair from a neighboring table. The legs scraped against the concrete floor as they situated themselves around the small table.

Kenny's red-rimmed eyes scanned the café, making certain they hadn't drawn any undue attention, and Logan's eyes narrowed suspiciously. He was grateful he had thought to stop and wire themselves with the small recording devices. He'd never let the Jukes get away with this, and he was determined to do everything in his power, once Zaza was safely in his arms, to see that justice was served. Logan's eyes scanned Kenny's face, and the older man licked his lips nervously before he handed Kadie and Beth a menu.

"Please, take time to order something." He encouraged, and Kadie glared.

"No, thanks," she spat.

Logan tore his eyes from Kenny's and glanced toward Kadie. She regarded the man with a fierce scowl, and Logan touched her shoulder gently.

"Go ahead, Kadie. You haven't had anything to eat in *days*," he stressed. He glanced meaningfully across the table.

Kenny paled, but he regained his composure when a waitress approached their small table with a smile. "Are you folks having a pleasant night? My name is Nancy. What can I get you today?"

Kadie's eyes narrowed when Logan ordered. "I'll have the pastrami and fries with a coke." He looked at her pointedly.

Her lips twisted with disdain before she ordered, "I'll have the fish and chips, please."

"And what to drink?" the waitress pressed.

"Orange soda."

"I'll have the same," Beth told the waitress.

The waitress turned her attention to Kenny, and he waved her off with a brush of his hand. "Nothing for me, thank you."

Nancy gave them a parting smile before she disappeared, leaving them alone with Kenny. Kenny smiled and spoke, "That's better isn't it?"

Logan's eyes shot to his. "Enough games, Jukes. I want answers—now!" His eyes turned dark, and his words were forceful.

Kenny took a deep breath, shaking his head slowly. "I'm afraid I don't have a lot to offer you." He spoke without malice, and Logan's face twisted.

"What do you mean?"

"I didn't know about . . . *this*," Kenny spread his hands wide. "I didn't know about any of this until earlier this afternoon."

Logan sat up straighter. "You—"

"Please," the man countered, "let me finish. I'll tell you all I know."

Logan felt Kadie's body stiffen next to his, and Beth looked ill. Kadie's skin paled, and she regarded Kenny with parted lips.

"Late last night, I heard my father awake in his office. I rose to see if he needed anything. When I neared the office, I overheard him talking to someone at the police station. He mentioned your name—" Kenny frowned. "I heard him say, 'If Matthews approaches your department, he'll never see his kid again.' My father told the recipient that if you did approach the police, his job was to keep it from the media and to 'take care' of you."

Logan's stomach turned and he closed his eyes as Kenny continued, "I have known my dad to play dirty before, and it came as no surprise that he had done . . . *something*. He was very upset after your visit. I didn't know what . . . . Well, I confronted him this morning. We argued. It was one of the worst arguments we have ever had. He told me to stay out of his way, but I kept at him until he talked. He told me what he'd done. He informed me he had dumped you and the woman in the middle of Olympic Park, and he confessed to taking your girl.

"He wouldn't tell me anything more. Then suddenly—he collapsed, and he hasn't awakened since. He cannot talk, he cannot respond, and . . . and he is the only one who knows where your daughter is."

"No!" Logan slammed his fists against the table. "No!" he ground out between tightly clenched teeth.

Several late-night diners looked their way, and Kenny glanced about nervously before he whispered, "Calm down. Now, I've spent all morning trying to figure out who he was working with, trying to get some answers. However, I'm afraid to say my father has many friends in low and *high* places. He has always played his dirty tricks close to the chest. Through the years, I've kept my mouth shut and turned a blind eye, but this . . . ?" He shrugged. "I'm trying my best to help you.

"However, you need to understand that *no one* else will help you. Like I said—friends in high places. I will do what I can, but if my father doesn't wake up . . . ." Kenny's voice faltered and he shook his head helplessly.

"No—no!" Logan's mind felt numb. His body quaked with grief. "You find the answers! You find her!"

Several people looked their way again, and Kenny eyed him meaningfully. "Anything you do—you will be arrested immediately. You'll lose any chance you have to find your daughter."

"There has to be a way. There just has to be," Kadie spoke hoarsely.

Kenny sighed. "I'm doing all I can. I'll keep trying, and in the meantime—all we can do is hope he wakes soon. I'm sorry. I truly am. But like I said—he has set things up nicely. One wrong move and any chance of finding your daughter is gone."

* * * * * * *

No, no, no . . . Kadie's mind felt like a broken record player. What was going to happen now? *Logan . . .* Her heart ached for him. Where was Zaza? How would they find her if no one but the senator knew where she was? *No, no, no!* She closed her eyes. She felt Logan's taut, trembling body next to hers. His fists were clenched. His muscles quivered.

She couldn't let him lose control. He had to stay in control or any chance they had to find Zaza would be lost. She believed Kenny. There would not be another chance, and time was against them. She took a deep breath and laid her hand against his strong forearm. His muscles jerked against her palm, and she squeezed gently.

"Then what do you suggest we do, Mr. Jukes?" Kadie pressed.

Logan's rage was evident in the strong lines of his face, and she could only trust he'd stay calm. Kenny Jukes glanced at Logan warily and answered, "I'm doing what I can. I will do my best, but in the meantime—go home. These people are not going to go down without a fight, and they will do what they need to do if they feel like you're able to expose them."

"I can't just leave my daughter out there! Someone has to know," Logan ground out. His voice trembled with barely restrained fury.

"He told me himself he was the only one who knew where she was. He did it himself and told no one. Go home—I'll do the best I can. That's all I can promise," Kenny replied. Kadie recognized regret in the timbre of his words, but it didn't lessen her pain.

"And in the meantime—I do what? I wait until someone finds my daughter's corpse?"

"Careful, Logan," Kenny cautioned. His eyes darted across the café. "I've told you all I can. Keep in mind—you won't do her any good behind bars, which is where you'll end up . . . or worse, son. Again, I'm sorry I can't be of more help. I must go now. I'll take care of the tab."

Kenny stood and smoothed the front of his business coat. He nodded curtly, his eyes not quite meeting Logan's as he turned to leave. Kadie watched with horrified eyes as the senator's son left the café and disappeared into the night.

"*Logan?*" Beth finally spoke. Tears coursed down her cheeks. She wiped at them with agitated hands.

"Let's go." Logan spoke. "We need to find help, and we can't do anything here."

* * * * * * *

Logan navigated Beth's modest sedan through the streets of Seattle. The silence that enveloped the car was frightening, and Kadie's heart felt as if it were breaking. Poor little Zaza. Where was the little girl? What were they to do? Logan looked nearly demented. His hair stood in untidy tufts, and his dark beard accentuated the pallor under his skin. His face was drawn, and his eyes were wild with warring emotions.

Kadie tried desperately to push back the immense feelings of despair and hopelessness as they loaded onto the ferry, docked at Seattle's port. A few tears pushed through her reserve and she wiped at them, feeling helpless. Why had she ever come? She couldn't imagine her life without Logan. Over the past few days they had become so close. Their lives were forever linked together, and she knew Logan Matthews was much more than a mere friend. She was in love with him. She knew it without a doubt, and that was why her coming had been so wrong. It was her fault Zaza was missing.

If she'd only listened to Maysha and stayed in Utah where she belonged, Logan's little girl wouldn't be gone. The mystery of the Clarke family's death would have remained buried and forgotten, just as it should have been. She should have never taken that can from that hole. It had lain among the ruins for years. If she had left well enough alone, Logan and his family would be safe. A soft moan tore from her throat, and her head hung with despair. She felt utterly remorseful, and guilt plagued her mind.

The car drove forward into the loading zone just as Beth turned in her seat to face Kadie. Kadie hardly dared meet Beth's tortured eyes, but Beth reached back to grasp her hand.

"We'll find her, Kadie," Logan's sister whispered. Then as if reading Kadie's thoughts she added, "If you and Maysha weren't here, I think I would just fall apart. I was so grateful Maysha was there with me through all of this, and to know Logan wasn't alone was such a comfort."

Kadie laughed mirthlessly and whispered, "If we hadn't come, Zaza would still be here."

Logan spun to face her. His hard eyes fell on hers, and he replied, "You are not going to blame yourself for this, Kadence Reynolds. Don't you dare. You and I talked about this before. Beth is right. Without you and Maysha . . . ." He closed his eyes. "Kadie, your strength has been mine," he finished.

Her eyes fell to the floor. "There has to be some way to find her. We have to find her." Her voice sounded tortured, strangled.

Logan nodded. "We will—we will find her." He sighed. "Do you want to go up top?" he directed to Beth.

Beth nodded. "I could use a restroom."

They exited the car and squeezed past the other vehicles parked on the massive boat. They climbed the stairs and came out on the deck where several passengers milled about. Some sat reading, while others leaned against the railings. Beth turned for the restroom while Logan and Kadie walked to the rails. Kadie watched the city lights shimmering on the waves. Moonlight bathed the sea in white, iridescent light. They stood silent. Each absorbed in their own tortured thoughts. Logan gazed off toward the horizon, and Kadie watched the dark waters. The current created by the boat caused little whirlpools, and she gazed into the water's inky depth. Then, without warning, there was a flash of white. Kadie let out a startled gasp as Charlotte's image seemed to materialize just below the surface, her body floating weightlessly on the waves.

Charlotte's white night dress floated out around her, cradling her body. Her long tresses fanned out from her pale face. Her eyes were closed. Kadie's astonished eyes shot to Logan. He remained focused on the horizon. Confused, she turned back toward the water. The image, just as the times before, was gone.

What do you want? Kadie demanded. *What do you want, Charlotte?* She feared she was going insane. She closed her eyes, and like a bolt of electricity the images from her dream shot to the forefront of her mind. Kadie inhaled deeply as the image assaulted her senses.

Charlotte stood high up on a ledge. The black waves broke against the yawning cliff face below her, sending tendrils of mist high into the air. She turned to face Kadie, her eyes pleading.

The image's clarity startled Kadie and suddenly she gasped. *The cliff. A cave!*

Her eyes shot open. "She's in a cave," she whispered. The words rushed from her lips, and she felt Logan turn toward her.

"What?" he asked.

Kadie's eyes narrowed in thought, and she wiped her clammy palms on the front of her jeans. Was it possible? Is that what Charlotte had been trying to tell her? She felt sure of the answer. The dream— it had seemed so real. Could it be? Kadie blanched. *What is going on?* Surely she was crazy. *It was only a dream, but what if . . . .* The last time she had seen Charlotte's image had been in the mist, in the mountains. She had felt the same unquestionable knowledge then. She'd felt sure she and Logan needed to follow that path.

Could it be Charlotte had led them in that direction? In the direction they needed to go to find help? Their path had led them to Mack, and if they had not found Mack, she and Logan would still be wandering in the wilderness, lost. Their fate may have been terrible. They could have been killed.

"Kadie?" Logan's voice broke through her chaotic thoughts.

"She's in a cave," she repeated, and the words felt right.

"How . . . ? Kadie . . . ."

Her incredulous eyes shot to his face. "Look, I know this sounds crazy . . . insane—but yesterday, in the woods . . . Logan, I *saw* Charlotte. *I saw her!* It was the same image I saw in the window in your office."

Logan's eyebrows rose skeptically, and his lips parted. "Kadie . . . ."

"And last night—" She rushed on. She tried to ignore his incredulous expression as she continued. "I dreamed of her. I saw her running in the hills above Eureka. The house was in flames below her, and she fell—deep into the darkness, and then—suddenly, she was standing on the edge of a cliff.

"The woods—these woods—" She waved her hand toward the shoreline. "Ferns, and hemlocks, and giant maples—they were behind her. There was a cave in the cliff face. She jumped! I saw the cave. Charlotte was floating in the water, and then I woke up," she finished breathlessly.

Logan shook his head and ran a hand across his bearded face. "Kadie, I . . . ."

"I know I sound crazy," she repeated, "and I promise I'll let you commit me when this is all over. But when we visited Senator Jukes' house, I remember seeing photos . . . pictures hanging in the hallway. They were *caves*, Logan. Senator Jukes, and his children, and his grandchildren were all dressed in spelunking gear. Harnesses and headlamps—and they were standing at the mouths of a dozen different caves. There were even photos of Senator Jukes inside the caves. He put Zaza in a cave!"

The color drained from Logan's face and he appeared even paler than before. His eyes were wide, and he swallowed hard. He ducked his head, his brows knit together in thought, and Kadie held her breath expectantly. Did he think she was delusional? Maybe she was, but she felt certain of her words. Her words felt right. *She was right.*

Logan took a deep breath, and his eyes met hers. "I . . . I don't know."

Kadie's heart constricted painfully and she frowned, trying not to focus on her fading pride. "Are there any caves around here, along the coastline?" she implored. "I know this sounds certifiably crazy, but I feel like she's showing us the way. I feel like I'm losing my mind at times, but she led us to Mack. She's showing us the way to Zaza."

"I don't know of any . . . I can't think of any caves along *this* coastline, Kadie. I've never heard of any sea caves nearby."

"Sea caves? You mean Totem cave?" Beth spoke from behind them, and they jumped, not prepared for her sudden arrival.

Her eyes were wide as she joined them at the rails. Confused, she glanced back and forth between Logan and Kadie. Kadie noted that Beth's face was red and swollen from tears. Instinctively, she reached out and laid a tentative hand on her new friend's shoulder. Beth placed her hand over top of Kadie's, holding her close.

Logan shook his head and asked, "Are there sea caves around here?"

Beth shrugged. "Yes, but only one that I know of. A few of the local kids from school knew about it. I went on a date with Chris Barlow, and he took us for a midnight picnic. He said it was haunted by the Squamish Indians who once lived in this area. Chris took us inside at low tide. Apparently there have been a few ancient artifacts found in the cave as well. There are some really unique petroglyphs on the walls of the right fork. I was terrified—the sounds in that cave . . . ." Beth shivered. "Brian Larson kept teasing, saying we would be trapped in at high tide. Apparently, the tide seals the entrance and the swells inside the cave are really strong. There's no hope of getting out until low tide."

Logan grasped her arm, his eyes wide. "Where is it?"

Beth looked between him and Kadie with a bewildered expression. "It's not too far from Grandma and Grandpa's old place. Why?"

Logan's eyes narrowed, and he regarded Kadie with a frown. She squirmed under his close scrutiny and her hands trembled. *Please believe me*, she pled silently.

"Zaza might be in that cave," he replied.

Beth's mouth fell open. "What makes you believe that? Did Kenny Jukes call?"

"No." Logan kept his gaze on Kadie's and she bit her bottom lip self-consciously. "We'll explain later. Can you take us there?"

"Now? In the dark?" Beth questioned. "I don't know if I'll find it."

"Try, please, Beth," Logan implored, turning to face his sister.

"Yes, of course. I'll do my best. Even if I have to go pound on Chris Barlow's door, we'll find it, okay?" she replied, and Kadie smiled her relief.

CHAPTER *Sixteen*

The drive back to the house seemed to take ages, and Kadie was grateful when they pulled onto the narrow lane leading to Logan's home. Logan pushed the little car at a terrifying speed down the road, and when he pulled into the circular drive, the tires squealed, disturbing the quiet of the early morning. The front porch light glowed, sending beams of orange light streaming across the porch and fanning out across the blacktop. The door flew open, and Maysha burst out of the house. She ran down the porch, nearly falling off the last stair.

"Maysha!"

A sob caught in Kadie's throat as she jumped from the car and caught her sister tightly against her. Beth moved closer, hesitantly, and Maysha reached out, grasping Logan's sister around the shoulder. She pulled her into the hug, and the three held each other tight for several long moments.

Kadie heard Logan clear his throat after long seconds had passed, and she glanced toward him. Their gazes held, and he stepped closer. He placed his hand on the small of Kadie's back, and she sighed, enjoying the warmth and comfort of his familiar touch. He kissed her temple gently and patted Maysha's shoulder.

"Thank you for taking such good care of Adelaide, Maysha. I'll . . . uh—go and get some gear together. If we hurry, we can make it before high tide."

Maysha pulled from Kadie's grasp and glanced back and forth between them as Logan stepped past them. He advanced up the porch and into the house. "Now what?" Maysha moaned.

Beth glanced uncertainly toward Kadie and replied, "We think Senator Jukes may have hidden Zaza in a sea cave, not too far from here."

Maysha scowled. "Unbelievable," she muttered.

"We don't know for certain if it's the right place or not," Kadie added.

"What do you mean?" her sister asked, confused.

Logan returned just then, carrying a backpack slung across one shoulder. He motioned toward the car. "We need to go now, before high tide."

He rushed to get behind the wheel and Kadie looked to her sister, her expression imploring. "We'll explain later, okay? We'll be back soon."

Maysha shoulders slumped, and she nodded. "Be careful," she whispered.

Kadie kissed her sister's cheek and followed Beth to the car. It didn't take long for Beth to direct Logan to an area of woods near the shoreline, several miles outside of town. The car jolted as it hit the potholes in the obscure road that lead through the thick forest. Logan's window was rolled down, and the sound of the roaring surf in the distance caused Kadie's hands to tremble. The headlights caught a small, black-tailed deer crossing the road, and Logan slowed momentarily, allowing the deer an opportunity to skitter off the path. It ran into the dense trees and disappeared behind a wall of ferns.

Kadie breathed in the briny, humid air. A wall of mist loomed ahead, and the hairs on her arm rose, her nerves on edge. *Please let it be so*, she thought. What if she were wrong? What if she really was going insane—then what? Were she and Logan risking high tide to explore an empty cavern? If the tide raised high enough to cut off the entrance, Kadie knew they'd have to wait several hours to get out. She closed her eyes and rested her chin against her chest. Her conviction that she was following the right prompting seemed strong, but what if. . . . She let the thought fall away. They had to check, regardless. What else were they to do but try?

The trees gave way as Logan turned into a wide, empty parking lot. The parking lot sat high on the cliffs. It overlooked the waters, and pockets of opaque mist shrouded the coastline. The scene was eerie, and the roar of the surf caused Kadie's heart to accelerate. They stepped from the car, and Logan grabbed the backpack. He tossed Kadie and Beth a flashlight. Kadie clicked her light on, and they worked their way down the slippery, wooden staircase that led to the sandy beach.

"It's just around this bend. The cliff is hidden in the mist," Beth spoke as they walked the edge of the shoreline.

The waves thundered ashore, and Kadie watched the high, cresting waves. The mist loomed like a brick wall in front of them, and she struggled to find the cliff face in the distance. Once they drew near, the mist faded enough for Kadie to make out the hazy outline of the precipice and the forest. She inhaled sharply. The air hissed through her nostrils. The haunting image was that of her dreams. She watched the edge of the cliff warily, half expecting to see Charlotte standing on the edge, but all remained still.

"It's there. You can see the opening. You have to stay as close to the rock face as possible. The tide is coming in. Are you sure about this?" Beth lamented.

"Here's the extra phone," Logan replied as he pulled a phone from his pocket. He handed it to his sister and glanced at Kadie. "I don't know if I'm going to make it in or out before high tide. I'll call when I'm in if I can. If you don't hear from me in two hours then call for help. If I don't get out, make a copy of the conversation with Kenny Jukes and give it to the sheriff. I don't care what Jukes says. Friends in high places or not, I'm going to get my daughter back."

Beth paled, and she nodded.

"Well, you're not going in there alone," Kadie spoke.

Logan's eyes met hers. "I don't know what I'm going to find. I don't know if I can get in or out. Stay here, please."

"No," she interjected. "I'm not going to wait here. I'm coming with you. I can help, Logan." His lips pressed together, and he shook his head. Kadie repeated, "I'm coming with you, whether you want me to or not. When this is over, then you can get rid of me, but for now, I'm staying with you."

Logan raked a hand through his hair, and his expression darkened. "Kadie . . . ." he scowled. Then, "Fine," he caved and his eyes found Beth's. "You'll be okay?"

"The tide is coming in fast. If you go in, you won't get out in time."

"I have to try. If my daughter is in there, I have to try," he returned. "Now, you'll be all right?"

Beth nodded. "Yes, I'll wait here." She touched Kadie's arm, pulling her in for a quick embrace. "Be careful," she whispered. She pointed ahead. "Just stick to the wall."

They wasted no time as they ran down the length of the beach toward the cliff looming ahead. Kadie tried to ignore the rushing swells, and she eyed the edge of the precipice with trepidation. Twisted, knotted pines reached toward the ocean. Their ancient roots spewed from the rock face, and moss hung in curtains from their branches.

She shivered when the deep, guttural sound of the waves echoing in the cavern met her ears, and she willed her mind to find courage. Logan followed the steep wall. She stayed close behind, and water rushed over her tennis shoes. The icy water flowed around her ankles, and she shuddered as another wave followed behind, soaking her to her knees.

"Careful. Watch the undertow, and keep your hands clear of the barnacles," Logan cautioned as they entered the mouth of the sea cavern.

The sound of the rushing water echoed deep from within, and Kadie shone her light on the walls as they sloshed through the foaming surf. Giant communities of barnacles glowed in the beam of her light, and brightly colored starfish clung to the wet walls and low ceiling. If a giant wave came in, they would surely drown. Her heart pounded in her ears, and she struggled to hear past the rush of blood in her head. Another wave crashed against the opening, and the water rose to her knees. She felt the strong undertow pulling against her legs. She swallowed her fear and pushed her way forward, following closely behind Logan.

"Zaza?" he called. His voice reverberated against the low ceiling. They paused for a moment to listen before they continued into the dark abyss. The water stayed ankle deep, and Kadie shivered when another wave thundered through the opening and water rushed to her thighs. She struggled against the undertow, and her heart pounded against her ribs. Would they be swallowed by the ever-rising tide?

Kadie took a ragged breath as Logan called for Zaza again. Only the sound of the deafening surf called back. The water level dropped as they moved further in, and Kadie breathed a little easier. Their lights reflected off the many colorful tidal pools, and she and Logan stepped across several pockets of deep water. Multi-hued anemones, small fish, and crabs inhabited the various pools.

Kadie trained her light on the ceiling above them, and she studied the starfish clinging to the rough, black stone. "Does the water go all the way to the ceiling?" she asked, her voice sounding breathless to her ears.

Logan paused and reached back for her hand. "The tide won't come in that fast. If we don't find dry sand soon, we'll get out before the tide gets too high. I'll help you swim out," he reassured her.

Another wave thundered in and swirled about Kadie's ankles. She focused on keeping her footing in the soft sand, and she paused when a sudden, shrill sound tore at her ears. The shriek caused cold fingers of fear to crawl along her spine.

"Did you hear that?" she breathed.

Logan paused and listened. He licked his dry lips. "The surf. Sounds echo in these caves."

Kadie swallowed hard. "I don't think . . . ."

He moved forward and shined his light on the ceiling. "I can see the tide line on the walls."

"The water can't reach this far in then?"

"No, the tide ends here."

She exhaled as she stepped across a thick layer of wet branches, pine cones, and dead, decaying sea life. The accumulation was covered in dirty, sticky foam, and it smelled sour. Kadie winced as she stepped onto drier sand, and her eyes darted around the dark cavern. The sound of the surf echoed eerily behind them, and another shrill, haunting shriek came from ahead.

"I heard that," Logan murmured.

Kadie tensed and gooseflesh rose across her arms. "What was that?"

"I'm not sure—Zaza?" he called.

They heard no answer, and he led them onto drier sand where the cave forked.

"This must be what Beth was talking about," Logan spoke as he trained his light on the right fork of the cave, then the left.

He stepped toward the right fork. His flashlight beam bounced off the narrow walls, and Kadie's eyes broadened when she noticed many petroglyphs carved deep into the wall. Eerie round faces and bulbous carved whales stared down at them. Kadie stepped into the entrance of the right fork and glanced about, amazed. The deep, guttural sound reverberated once again from the left fork. Jumping back, she stumbled into Logan. His hand shot out and he steadied her before his light shot to the left fork.

"What *is* that?" she whispered. "Is that Zaza?"

"No. Whatever it is, it isn't human."

Logan stepped toward the narrow opening of the left fork. The darkness swallowed his light, and Kadie held her breath expectantly. A cold breeze brushed across her cheek, and she shivered.

They waited in tense silence for several moments before Kadie asked, "Which way do you want to go? That way?" She pointed hopefully toward the right fork. *The tunnel that doesn't emit ghostly moans*, she thought.

Logan's brow furrowed while he contemplated their next move. After a moment, he shook his head. "No, I want to go this way."

With a determined expression, he stepped into the narrow tunnel. Kadie hesitated. Her breath came in shallow gasps. Fear clouded her mind, and she took a deep breath just as a loud, deafening roar filled the cave. A startled scream tore from her throat, and she spun around just in time to see an immense, dark wall of water barreling toward them. With no time to run, she covered her head with her arms, and her shrill scream was cut short as the wave hit her full force. The force of the water knocked her feet out from beneath her. Salt water filled her mouth and nose as she was picked up and slammed into the stone wall.

Sharp barnacles pierced her skin, and she struggled against the fury of the rushing water. Her head surfaced. With only a moment to spare, she gulped a lung full of air before another swell buried her head. The strong current pulled her under. Struggling for air, Kadie pushed against the force, and her mind screamed in horror as she realized the current was pulling her to sea. She kicked with all her strength, and her lungs felt as if they would burst into flames. *I'm dying! I'm dying! I can't die!* Her mind repeated as she contended with the current.

Another incoming wave sent her body barreling forward. Kadie struggled to find air. The strong wave slammed her body up against the craggy wall once again, knocking the breath from her. She gulped a mouth full of searing salt water. Light exploded behind her eyes. Suddenly, strong arms caught her tightly about the waist, and she gasped when her head surfaced above the water. Logan pulled her through the churning current. Kadie barely registered the sand under her feet.

"Keep going!" Logan's voiced echoed off the narrow walls, and he dragged her across the sand. "Come on!" He jerked her to her feet. With great effort, Kadie forced her legs to move. A weak scream burst from her trembling lips when another wave roared overhead, knocking both her and Logan down. Water surged over their heads, but Logan's strong grasp held fast, and he stood, pulling her with him.

"Further in! Come on, Kadie. Move!" he screamed, and Kadie stumbled behind him. Logan's flashlight's beam danced against the narrow walls as they rushed up the left fork. Kadie could hear the thunder of waves behind them, and she forced her legs to keep moving.

Her lungs burned and her body trembled violently when they finally collapsed onto dry sand. Logan faced the way they'd come and he watched the waves swell at the mouth of the left fork. He groaned and fell back into the soft sand.

"We're safe here." He breathed and turned to Kadie.

Kadie trembled. Her stomach rolled. She coughed violently, and her throat and lungs felt as if they were on fire. Logan pounded her back with the palm of his hand, and she grasped her heaving stomach. Rolling to her knees, she vomited seawater onto the sand. Sharp, itchy particles of sand clung to her face, neck, and body, but she paid them no mind as she took several gulping breaths. Logan crawled next to her, and he wrapped his arms around her quaking body.

"Shhh—we're okay, now. You're safe," Logan soothed. With a strangled cry, she buried her face in his neck. "We're safe, honey.

I have you—we're safe now." He continued to murmur softly against her ear.

He held her for several long moments until her violent trembling and quiet sobs subsided. "We're—we're safe here?" Her teeth chattered.

Logan glanced back into the pitch-black tunnel. The sound of the surf echoed as it rushed into the cavern. "Yes, we're safe here. We went up an incline once we managed to get further in." He brushed the sand from his off his flashlight and focused the beam on the walls.

He sat up, pulling her with him. She let him assist her to a sitting position, and he swept the light across her sodden body. Dark, crimson blood ran in rivulets down her forearm, and Logan's lips pressed together. Kadie brushed at the sand clinging to the abrasions, and she hissed when the pain began to register. The salt burned the shallow cuts, and she gritted her teeth when Logan used the tail of his shirt to remove the remaining sand.

"You must have cut yourself on a colony of barnacles when the wave threw you against the wall. I'd have never been able to reach you if it hadn't," Logan spoke. His voice echoed in the narrow cavern.

"I thought I was being sucked out to sea," she murmured.

"You would have—the tide shouldn't have come that far in. Those were what we call sneaker waves. They're dangerous even at the best of times. The tide must have come in higher than usual. It happens. If there is a storm near the Alaskan gulf, we get high breakers during high tide. It doesn't usually happen this time of year. We're just lucky to have been in as far as we were when it hit. Kadie, I'm sorry. I should have never let you come."

"I'm fine," she replied, attempting to control her emotions.

Logan raked his hand through his wet hair. "We need to get out of here."

Just then another thin, grating whine echoed from ahead. Frightened, Kadie rolled onto her knees. She tensed as Logan trained his light into the narrow tunnel ahead. The thick darkness swallowed the beam and another draft brushed past their sodden bodies. The sound echoed louder.

"What . . . Logan, what is that?" she whispered. She tried to stand,

and Logan grasped her elbow gently. He assisted her to her feet.

"I don't know, but it isn't human."

The deep thunder of the surf roared behind them, and she turned to glance back the way they had just come. Her heart hammered against her chest. The tunnel was inky black. "You don't th—think Zaza would have tried to swim out—out of that?"

"I hope not," he breathed. "She's old enough to know when the tide is high, but it's so dark . . . ," Logan replied. "Can you manage to walk? There has to be an opening further in. There's a draft."

"And a sea monster?" Kadie added humorlessly.

"There's only one way to find out, huh?" Logan murmured, holding fast to Kadie's arm.

He led them deeper into the narrow passageway, and Kadie followed closely. The sand was soft and difficult to walk on, but she forced her rubbery legs to move forward. The further they traveled, the narrower the walls became. Kadie swallowed her claustrophobia. The passageway had just enough room to clear their shoulders and soon it became necessary to turn sideways.

She tucked her shoulder blades back to keep from scratching her skin on the coarse walls, and she took another calming breath. The grating sound echoed down the tunnel once more. Logan paused momentarily before he moved forward again. Soon, the pathway widened, and Kadie released a pent-up breath when the walls drew further apart. The sand was still soft, but she was surprised when broken shells crunched under foot. Logan swept the ground with the beam of his light, and her nose twitched when an unfamiliar, musky scent assaulted her.

"Sea lions," Logan whispered.

"Are they dangerous?"

"Not really. We'll be careful," he replied as they moved into a narrow, high-ceilinged cavern.

He frowned when he realized their path was blocked by several large boulders. Deep tracks showed in the sand and Logan followed the tracks to a small opening at the base of the rock wall.

"There are sea lions," he noted as he bent and tried to sweep the sand back from the opening. "We can't dig it. The ground is solid under the sand."

He raked a hand through his wet hair. Sand particles clung to his dark, wet locks. Logan suddenly cursed and slammed the ground with his fist.

Kadie studied the top of the wall, and then spoke, "Can we get over the top?"

"What are the chances they would bring Zaza here? The fork is under water. We can't back track—not until the tide goes down. We're stuck in here."

Kadie's eyes narrowed and she moved to the wall. Her teeth clamped together, and she willed her body to stop trembling. She wouldn't give up now. They had to go forward. She felt sure of it. She forced her weak legs to steady her, and she began climbing the boulders, carefully. "Logan, help me up," she called.

Logan groaned, but stood and steadied her. "Kadie, be careful. If that wall gives—"

"I'll be careful."

It took only moments to reach the top, but her fingers and legs ached with strain, and her breath was short and ragged. It taxed her already expended energy to pull her body weight up high enough to peer through the narrow opening between the wall and the ceiling. She paused to catch her breath, then reached for Logan's flashlight.

"I need the light."

She strained her arm to reach the flashlight he held toward her. A small rock came loose. It echoed as it tumbled down the wall, and Kadie cringed when Logan ducked his head under his arm to avoid a shower of smaller pebbles.

"Sorry!"

"Be careful. Don't get hurt," Logan cautioned.

With shaking arms, she pulled her head and shoulders through the tight gap. The sharp stone wall cut into her back as she pulled the flashlight around to examine other side of the blockage. Nervously, she peered over the edge. The light illuminated a small round cavern, and Kadie gasped loudly. She flipped the light off. A ghostly, opaque glow spilled from a small opening at the base of the wall.

The light was not bright enough to illuminate more than a few feet ahead of the opening, but the hole looked large enough for both her and Logan to squeeze through. There had to be a way out of the cave on the other side. She flipped the flashlight on again and swept the bright beam around the cavern. The cavern contained no signs of animal life besides the tracks left in the sand by sea lions.

She wiggled her body a bit more and squeezed through the gap. "There's an opening on this," she called.

Being careful not to bring the entire wall crashing down, Kadie worked to dislodge two larger boulders. The sound of stone hitting stone pierced her ears, and Logan's voice yelled across the clamor, "Kadie!"

"I'm fine!" She called to reassure him. She cleared a space big enough to squeeze through and descended the short rock wall, careful to keep a tight hold on the flashlight. Her muscles shook as she dug her fingers against the rock to keep from falling, and she gasped when she dislodged another bowling ball-sized rock. It tumbled to the cavern floor with a deafening clatter. She froze.

"Are you all right?" Logan's frantic voice echoed against the walls.

"Yes," she called. "I just knocked another rock loose. This side isn't as stable. Be careful."

"You too. I'm coming right behind you. I'll wait to descend until you're safely down."

When she reached the bottom, she turned her flashlight to the ceiling. The beam caught Logan's face and reflected against his dark eyes. Kadie held her breath as he squeezed through the narrow gap. His broad shoulders barely cleared the opening.

"Stand back in case I knock a stone loose," he cautioned.

Kadie moved toward the wall on the opposite side and watched as Logan twisted his body at a strange angle to clear the hole. A few smaller stones broke loose. She stepped back further to allow the light to shine in a larger arch, and she smiled weakly when he dropped down in front of her. He turned to face her, and she handed him the flashlight before she moved toward the opening in the wall. A gust of air burst through the hole and she shivered.

Logan joined her near the opening. A deep, long whine sounded loudly from the opposite side of the wall. She jumped back. Logan pushed her behind him and crouched near the base of the gap.

"I can't see anything," he whispered and then began digging the sand at the opening. Kadie moved to help him, and they shoveled the soft sand behind them to make the opening deeper. Logan ducked his head near the hole and again peered in.

"There's natural light coming in through the ceiling further back. It's not very light yet, and I can't see very far in," he told her.

He dropped down onto his stomach and worked his way through the fissure. His head disappeared, and darkness closed around Kadie as his body blocked all light.

"Be careful."

His feet slid through the hole, and he disappeared. Kadie dropped to her stomach and quickly followed. Once through the hole, she stood, and Logan grasped her elbow to steady her in the soft sand. He swept the flashlight across the large cavern. A fresh breeze brushed across their bodies, and Kadie gasped when his light rested on a large seal, standing in the middle of the grotto. The light reflected in its large eyes. The sea lion eyed them warily and barked. The animal opened its mouth wide and swayed back and forth, a quiet whine vibrating in its throat. Kadie was surprised to see two small seal pups a little further back. The light reflected off their wide, black eyes.

"Zaza?" Logan whispered. He stumbled forward, and Kadie gasped when the glow of his flashlight illuminated a dirty bundle of blankets tucked between the two pups.

Kadie's hands flew to her mouth, and she stifled a gasp. The flashlight dropped from Logan's fingers, and he rushed forward.

"Zahara!" His voice echoed in the cavern, and the mother seal barked a warning.

"Daddy?" a quiet voice called.

"Oh!" Kadie cried when the bundle of blankets moved. Zaza's little head popped into view. Her eyes were wide and sleepy, and her dark hair was matted against her skull and forehead. "Zaza," Kadie spoke the little girl's name. She looked on incredulously as Logan caught his little girl in his arms.

The seal pups whined and they scattered, scooting toward their mother. Kadie regarded the large animal with wary eyes as the family of seals moved to the opposite side of the cavern.

"Daddy!" Zaza's voice echoed in the cave.

Logan cradled his daughter in his arms. "My baby girl." He buried his face in Zaza's matted, sand-covered hair. His voice broke with emotion.

Kadie watched from a distance. She wanted to give them time for such an emotional reunion, and she bent to retrieve the flashlight Logan had dropped in the sand. The grotto was beginning to fill with the hazy light of early morning, but visibility in the cavern was still low. She shined the light toward the family of seals who watched them cautiously from the opposite wall.

She moved the beam around the large room, and Kadie's teeth ground together when the light caught an empty cooler, tipped onto its side. Empty chip bags, discarded juice boxes, and candy wrappers littered the ground. Broken crayons lay in the sand among the crushed shells and twigs. Kadie's face twisted. Anger at Senator Jukes boiled to the surface. How could someone leave a child in such conditions?

"Kadie!" Zaza's voice suddenly broke into her thoughts.

She turned just as Zaza bolted across the cavern and ran into her arms. She caught the girl with a joyous laugh, and Zaza wrapped her skinny arms about her neck. Kadie's eyes burned with unshed tears.

"I'm so glad you're safe," she whispered.

"You're all wet, just like Daddy." The little girl laughed as she pushed back to look into Kadie's tear-stained face. She reached her fingers to Kadie's wet eyes and smiled sweetly. "Don't cry, Kadie."

"I've just missed you," she whispered.

Zaza grinned her achingly familiar, toothless grin. "Me too!" She squirmed to get down, and Kadie released her. Zaza bounded back toward her father, and Kadie and Logan's eyes met in silent understanding. He smiled over the top of Zaza's head as he grasped his little girl against him.

"Aren't you cold, Daddy?" Zaza asked, hugging him.

He grinned and nodded. "I am. Are you?"

She nodded. "Yes."

He smiled and turned to Kadie. "There's enough wood down here to make a small fire. Zaza's right. We should get dry."

The mother seal barked again. Kadie jumped and Zaza laughed, covering her ears. "Quiet, Martha!" she hollered.

Kadie suddenly grinned and Logan laughed. "Martha?"

Zaza nodded. "Yep, the mama's Martha and the babies are Abigail and Gabriella," she announced and pointed at the pups. The mother seal barked again, and Zaza giggled. "It's okay, Martha. This is my daddy and my Kadie."

Kadie's heart warmed at being Zaza's 'Kadie,' and she smiled at the little girl. She could scarcely believe they had Zaza back again. Finding Zahara was a miracle. Zaza was safe. Kadie began gathering wood, and Logan stood to help. Zaza drew closer to the seal family, and the mother seal came near.

"Careful, Zaza," Logan cautioned.

Zaza bent and grabbed a larger stick. She brought it to Kadie with a smile. "It's okay, she won't hurt me. She thinks I'm one of her babies. That mean old man put me down in this hole with a rope. I was really scared, but the mama seal and her babies came. I thought she was going to bite me, but she ate my crayons instead. She spit them out 'cuz they tasted nasty."

The mother seal barked again. Zaza laughed and rushed to Logan's side. She grasped his large hand and continued, "That mean man came back once, and the mama seal tried to bite him." She laughed, and Logan swung her up in his arms.

"Zaza," he murmured against her soft cheek.

"I was really scared, Daddy. The lady said you'd come and get me, but you didn't come for a long time," Zaza replied.

"I'm sorry, baby," Logan choked on a sob and squeezed Zaza tightly. Then he asked, "What lady, Zaza?"

"The white lady." She shrugged. "She had on a long dress, and she came when it was dark, when I was the scaredest. She stayed with me while I fell asleep. She said you would find me and to be brave."

Kadie's face paled, and Logan met her gaze over the top of Zaza's head. They stared at one another in mute shock.

"You're choking me!" Zaza giggled against Logan's neck, and he tore his gaze from Kadie's. He laughed tersely and released her. She slid to the sand with a happy grin. "I'm cold. Will you make a fire now?"

CHAPTER *Seventeen*

*K*adie's eyes grew heavy while they sat around the small driftwood fire in comfortable silence. Zaza sat in the circle of Logan's arms while Kadie stretched her stiff muscles. Her clothes were dry and rigid with salt, and the sun streaming in from the small opening overhead filled the cavern with light. She watched Zaza, and she sighed when the little girl's eyes began to droop.

"You're sleepy," she whispered, and Zaza smiled tiredly.

"Go to sleep." Logan cuddled his daughter closer and Zaza yawned.

"You won't leave?" she asked sleepily.

Logan's jaw clenched, and tears rimmed his eyes. "Never," he spoke.

Zaza looked to Kadie. "You either? Don't go away, 'kay?" she yawned again, and Kadie swallowed the lump in her throat.

"I'll be here, Zaza." Her voice broke with emotion, and she watched with a full heart when Zaza turned into Logan's arms and closed her eyes.

They sat in silence for a long while before Logan moved. He shifted Zaza out of his arms gently to lay her on the blanket, then he pulled the excess up around his daughter's shoulder. He kissed her forehead tenderly before he stood and stretched his broad shoulders. Kadie's heart skipped a beat when he came to sit next to her on the soft sand. He placed his arm around her shoulders and pulled her against him.

"Thank you," he whispered. He pressed his lips to her forehead.

183

She relaxed against his side and laid her head against his shoulder. The mother seal barked, and Kadie watched as she ushered her two pups toward the fissure in the wall. The pups disappeared through the hole and the mother moved to follow.

"Thank you," Logan spoke to the animal. Kadie laughed, and Logan's eyes filled with humor. "You converse with ghosts. I talk to animals. I think they'll have us both committed." He chuckled.

"Definitely." Her smile broadened into a grin.

Logan exhaled, and his smile faded. "I can't thank you enough."

She shook her head and bit her bottom lip. "I didn't do anything. Charlotte—"

Logan's lips pressed together. "You listened."

"Thank you for saving me back there," she added. She suppressed a shiver as she thought about her close escape from the tide. "You saved me—back in the water. I thought . . . I thought I was going to die. And I thought, if I die . . . I kept thinking . . . ," She paused and took a deep breath. "I kept thinking, I'll never see him again," she finished with a whisper.

Logan tensed, and with worried eyes, Kadie raised her eyes to meet his. Emotion darkened his gaze. "Kadie." He spoke her name gently, and her heart quickened at the sound of her name on his lips.

He leaned in and kissed her on the mouth. His lips tasted of the sea, and he enveloped her trembling body in his arms as his kiss deepened ever so slightly. Kadie felt as if she were drowning in a tide of emotions. No one had ever tugged at her heart the way Logan did. Tears threatened as his kiss turned soft and searching, and she sighed. She knew without a doubt she loved Logan Matthews.

His lips dropped from hers, and he kissed her forehead before he smiled into her eyes. With one hand, he reached to wipe the dampness from her cheeks. "Try to get some rest," he murmured as he pulled her against his chest and held her.

She turned her face into his chest. All the emotions she'd experienced over the last few tumultuous days spilled over—her love for Logan, her fears, her doubts, and her joy at finding Zaza at last. She felt overwhelmed. Logan held her in the comforting circle of his arms for several long moments, and she took comfort in his warmth and strength. She listened to the sound of his heartbeat, the rush of the ocean in the distance, and the soothing noise of the crackling fire, mixed with Zaza's soft breaths. The arrangement created a sweet melody.

She never wanted to leave this; Logan and Zaza and spending time together was all she had ever wanted. It was all she would ever want. The thought made her heart ache. She and Maysha would have to leave and then . . . She closed her eyes and tried not to let doubts crowd the joy of the moment. The knowledge that their lives had touched at all was a miracle, and she was grateful for the time she had with them.

Logan continued to hold Kadie. His arms and the sweet ambience lulled her thoughts, and her eyes grew heavy. She was just beginning to doze when he grew tense. Startled, her eyes shot opened and she bolted out of his arms.

"What is it?" she asked.

Logan pushed her from his arms and stood. Kadie strained her ears, wondering if Senator Jukes' men had come looking for them. A distant sound met her ears, and he stepped into the bright stream of light pouring in overhead.

He brought his hands to his mouth and yelled, "We're here! We're down here!"

Kadie moaned her relief when she finally recognized the sound of Beth's shrill voice in the distance. Zaza stirred when Logan called again, and the little girl sat up with confused, frightened eyes.

"Daddy? Kadie?" she asked.

Kadie stepped over to the little girl and put a comforting arm around her. "It's okay, Zaza. There are people looking for us."

"Good people?" she whispered, and Kadie's heart twisted.

"Yes, I think it's Aunt Beth."

"We're here! Down here!" Logan hollered again. His voice bounced off the walls.

The voices calling from above drew closer. "Kadie? Logan?" Beth's familiar voice floated into the grotto.

"Here! Beth—we're here. Down here!" Logan responded again.

Kadie felt her knees grow weak when Beth's face appeared over the opening. She turned from the hole. "They're here! Hurry quickly!

They're here! Kadie! Logan! Are you all right?" Beth leaned into the hole. Her voice echoed in the cavern.

Kadie met Logan's eye and she smiled before she answered, "We're great, Beth."

"Aunt Beth!" Zaza crowed. She ran to Logan and wrapped her arms around her father's leg and jumped up and down.

"Zaza!" Beth called. "Oh, Logan! You found her! You found her!"

Men's voices drew near, and Kadie joined Zaza and Logan. He wrapped an arm around her shoulder and kissed her briefly. A man's head appeared in the opening, and Kadie's eyes widened. She exhaled sharply and stepped back, startled, when she recognized Kenny Jukes.

"Logan, we'll get you out of there as quick as we can. You three hang on. Don't worry. You're all safe now, and we've brought the sheriff."

Kadie felt oddly numb as the sheriff and his men lifted her, Logan, and Zaza from the cavern. Hands grasped her arms, brushed at her legs, and she felt Beth's arms wrap briefly around her shoulders before the Sheriff's men separated her and Logan. They quickly ushered Kadie through the thick woods toward a waiting line of police cruisers. She stared out of the car's window as an officer drove her to the police station in silence. When she walked into the office, her eyes widened as she caught sight of Maysha. Falling into her sister's arms, Kadie asked, "What happened? How did they find us?"

Maysha clasped Kadie's hand in hers. "You'd been gone *forever*, and I about died when Beth came home without you. She said a wave sealed off the entrance of that stupid cave, and she called the cops. I thought you *died*!" Her sister accused, her voice rising angrily before she went on. "Beth told the police everything, then that Jukes guy showed up right when the police did, and they all ran off to find Zaza. He said he knew where that senator had taken her. Beth called when they found you, then a nurse came to replace me, and they hauled me here for questioning."

"Yes," an officer spoke behind them. "And you've been *very* helpful." Kadie spun to face him. Maysha rolled her eyes, and the officer smirked, then waved his hand toward an empty room. "We know most of what happened, but we need your statement. We have men questioning Logan Matthews and Kenny Jukes."

"And Zaza?" Kadie asked.

"She's on her way to a nearby hospital. She needs to be checked out. Most likely, they'll release her tonight. Her Aunt Beth is with her."

With a heavy sigh, Kadie closed her eyes briefly before she stepped into the room.

* * * * * *

Logan sat quietly, staring out across the yard down toward the beach. The water sparkled in the brilliant afternoon sun, and a slight breeze blew in across the sea. He closed his eyes and listened to the gentle waves as he relaxed in the sun that warmed his shoulders. It was hard to imagine all that had happened over the last few days. He stiffened when he recognized the familiar sound of footsteps in the hallway. The glass doors slid open, and Logan stood. He turned to face his sister and Doctor Lowery.

Beth's face looked grim, and Logan greeted the old doctor with a firm handshake. "How is she?" he asked, already fearing the worst.

Doctor Lowery shook his head. "She's tired. I'm afraid to say, she won't be with us much longer. I hate to tell you such news after all you've been through, Logan." Logan exhaled and he nodded. Doctor Lowery frowned and placed a hand against Logan's shoulder. "I'll go ahead and show myself out," he replied. He turned and patted Beth's shoulder before he left.

Logan stepped back across the deck. He placed his hands on the railing and gazed back out toward the sea. His thoughts were troubled, and he moaned. He heard Beth step behind him.

"Kadie and Maysha are here. I heard their car pull in a minute ago," she spoke.

He nodded silently, but some of the tension in his shoulders drained away. Just the thought of seeing Kadie . . . . He sighed. Kadie and Maysha had left yesterday afternoon for their motel. After the sheriff and his men had lifted Logan, Kadie, and Zaza from the cavern, they had been separated for questioning. Logan had discovered that Kenny Jukes had finally been able to resolve where the senator had left Zaza. Adam Jukes still remained in a coma, but Kenny had been able to unravel the senator's plot, and several men were headed to prison.

The interrogations had lasted long into the day, and Logan had been anxious to bring Zaza home from the hospital where they'd taken the little girl to be examined. Zaza, besides a few bumps and bruises, had been in good health, and she'd been released later that evening. When he, Beth, and Zaza had finally returned home, Logan had discovered a note informing him Kadie and Maysha would stop by the house before they left for Utah. The thought of Kadie leaving left him terribly depressed.

"Logan?" Beth asked behind him.

"I heard you," he answered. He turned around to face Beth.

"Adelaide wants to talk with you and Kadie. I told her I would send you both in." She paused, then, "I'm afraid, Logan. I'm afraid she isn't going to last long at all. I've never seen her so weak and pale. She really is going, isn't she?" Beth's voice cracked and she glanced at Logan with tear-filled eyes.

Logan pulled his sister into an embrace. "She's lived a good life, Beth. And she's missed Grandpa terribly. But I'll miss her too—so much. She's been good to us."

His sister pulled from his embrace just as the doorbell sounded. Its familiar chimes echoed in the house. "She won't be the only person you'll miss," Beth sniffed. "Are you really going to let Kadie go?" Logan ran his hand across his freshly shaven jaw, and Beth smiled when the door bell chimed again. "I'll get it."

Logan turned back to face the view. Was he really going to let Kadie go? How could he stop her? She lived and worked in Utah. He had a career and home in Washington. *Besides*, he thought despondently, *she's only known me for a few crazy days.* He knew he loved her. It surprised him how natural it felt. It was as if he had known and loved her all his life. He didn't want her to go, but what right did he have to ask her to stay? He stared out at the glistening water for a few more moments before Beth's voice interrupted his depressed musing.

"Maybe you and Kadie should go and see Adelaide now. I'm going to go and call Jace," she spoke.

He turned to face her. Kadie stood behind Beth, and Logan and Kadie's gazes locked.

"Hi," she spoke.

"Kadie . . . ." He stepped toward her, taking her hand in his.

* * * * * * *

The sound of the oxygen machine saturated Adelaide's room, and the bright sunlight, spilling through the window, did little to dispel Kadie's gloom. Her eyes immediately fell on Adelaide's frail frame. Adelaide leaned against several pillows. Her breathing was harsh and labored. Her eyes were closed, and Kadie exhaled quietly when Logan reached over to touch the woman's frail, bony hand. Adelaide's eyes opened.

"Logan?" she whispered as her weak smile fell adoringly on her grandson. He reached out and took her frail hand into his. "You're such a good boy. I love you so," she finished before her gaze enveloped Kadie.

Kadie smiled, and Adelaide raised her free hand toward her. With a smile, she stepped forward and took Adelaide's hand in hers. Adelaide squeezed Kadie's hand, and her attention returned to Logan.

"Grandma—" Logan bent and kissed Adelaide's forehead. "I love you." He swallowed hard. "You and Grandpa . . . all that you did for us. Thank you. I haven't told you often enough how I love you and how much we appreciate you."

Adelaide smiled. "You didn't have to. I knew."

His lips pressed together and emotion filled his dark eyes. Adelaide's gaze moved back toward Kadie and she whispered, "You came here for a reason, Kadence. You were meant to find one another. Take care of each other. And, Logan?" Adelaide looked to Logan. "Don't give up on love, Logan."

Weakly, she pulled Kadie's hand toward his. She placed his hand on top of Kadie's, and Kadie's and Logan's eyes met momentarily. Adelaide's grasp grew weak, and Kadie's lips trembled as she studied the older woman's face. Adelaide's eyes closed, and she whispered, nearly inaudible, "Fred . . . Charlotte . . . ."

The medical equipment continued to sound, but Kadie knew

in that moment that Adelaide was gone. Tears rolled silently down Kadie's cheeks, and she watched Adelaide's face relax in death. She appeared to be sleeping. A soft sob tore from Kadie's throat when Logan whispered, "She's gone."

His hand tightened against her fingers for a brief moment before he pulled their hands out from underneath Adelaide's. He laid Adelaide's hands in her lap and leaned in to kiss his grandmother's forehead gently. "Goodbye. I love you," he whispered before he stood straight.

"Goodbye," Kadie whispered and she brushed a tear from off her chin.

They were together again, Charlotte and Adelaide.

Kadie felt Logan step closer, and she raised her eyes to his. He smiled and cupped her wet cheek with the palm of his hand. He wrapped one arm around her and pulled her in against him for a brief moment.

"She's right, you know," he whispered. "I need to let Beth know."

His arms dropped from around her, and he left the room silently. Kadie turned once more to face Adelaide. "Thank you," she spoke into the stillness. "I hope you and Charlotte have such joy in finding one another again."

A ray of sunlight spilled into the room, and Kadie felt Charlotte's familiar presence once more. The silver pendant on Adelaide's chest gleamed in the bright rays, and the sound of Charlotte's now-familiar voice whispered through the room. *"Adelaide . . . ."*

Kadie smiled. *Charlotte*, Kadie thought. *Thank you for showing us the way.* She closed her eyes briefly as she turned and left the room.

* * * * * * *

Maysha held on to Beth's hand as the hearse pulled away. Logan's sister sobbed quietly and Kadie watched with mixed emotions as the sleek, black vehicle circled the drive and disappeared down the wooded lane. The sigh of the wind in the trees and the sound of the surf caressed the house. Beth sniffed loudly, and Maysha caught Kadie's eye. A caring smile touched her sister's lips and few tears slipped down Maysha's cheeks.

Maysha wrapped her arm around Beth's shoulder. Kadie knew

Maysha and Beth had grown close during the last few days. Kadie also knew Maysha would miss Adelaide as well. Her sister had hardly left Adelaide's bedside while Beth had helped her and Logan. Zaza moved next to Kadie. Kadie smiled when she felt the little girl's hand slip into hers.

"I'm going to miss Grandma," she whispered.

"Me too," Kadie replied. She squeezed Zaza's hand tenderly.

"We'll all miss her." Logan moved forward and his arm wrapped around Kadie's waist. His eyes were on the wooded lane.

"She's at peace." Beth sniffed just as the sound of a car approaching drew their attention.

Logan pulled his arm from Kadie's waist, and he stepped down the porch when the car appeared. It drove the length of the drive slowly and parked just below the wide stairs. Kadie's mouth twisted curiously, and then she started with abrupt recognition when Kenny Jukes stepped from the back seat. Beth frowned, and Logan paused on the bottom stair.

"What does *he* want now?" Beth voiced.

"He did his best to help," Logan reminded them.

Kadie moved down the stairs and Maysha came to her side. "Who is it?" she asked.

"Kenny Jukes."

Maysha's face contorted with rage. Her fists clenched into balls, and she moved past Kadie with deliberate steps. Kadie jumped forward and grasped her sister's arm, pulling her back.

"I'm going to strangle him!" Maysha ground out between clenched teeth.

"Later. Anyway, it was the senator who did this," Kadie shushed her sister and she struggled to hear Kenny Jukes. "Stay here. I mean it, Maysha," she warned and moved closer to Logan.

"I'm sorry to have come at such a time like this. I saw the hearse. I'm assuming Adelaide Clarke has passed?" Kenny stepped toward Logan with a frown.

Logan nodded. "What do you want?" he asked gruffly, and Kenny held his hand up resignedly.

"My father died last night. I wanted you to know that I truly am sorry for the grief my father has caused you and your family, both old and new. I have . . . something that you may find interesting. I'm afraid to say it is a bit disturbing as well." He pulled a small book from his expensive suit coat and stepped toward Logan.

Logan eyed Kenny Jukes suspiciously, but he accepted the book and turned it around in his large hands as the man continued, "You'll find the answers you're looking for. It's the least my family can do for yours. I've marked the place. Do what you will with the information in that journal. It will all come public in the end, after all. Again, I am sorry for your loss. Good day." He nodded and waved a hand in farewell toward Kadie.

She raised her hand briefly as he slid into his Jaguar. The car circled the drive and disappeared down the wooded lane. Kadie raised a hand to her throat as her heart rate calmed, and she breathed slowly.

"Logan, what is it?" Beth joined them at the foot of the stairs.

Logan tore his eyes off the lane and looked down at the hardcover book in his hands. He flipped it open. "It's a journal," he replied.

"Oh, no! Not *another* journal," Maysha exclaimed irreverently.

Logan smiled wryly. "Why don't we all go inside?" he suggested, and he shut the book with a loud thump.

Kadie nodded, and she grasped Zaza's hand as they moved into the house. They stepped into the hallway, and Kadie couldn't help notice how lonely the house felt without Adelaide's presence. She felt Logan's hand on the small of her back as he came up behind her.

"Zaza?" Logan began.

"I know—I know. 'Go play in your room.'" She mimicked Logan perfectly, and he laughed.

"Yes, please. We won't be long, princess."

Zaza glanced at Kadie and frowned before she sulked upstairs. Kadie laughed quietly and followed Logan, Beth, and Maysha into the sitting room. Maysha slumped onto the worn leather sofa, and Kadie sat next to her sister. Beth pushed in beside Kadie and reached for her hand while Logan pulled the recliner closer to the couch. He sat in the rocker and opened the book to the page Kenny Jukes had marked. He began reading aloud, his voice deep and low:

"March twenty-first, 1995. My dreams have haunted me of late. I continually see her face. So I write this in the hope that I will one day find peace from my sins. No one must ever know. My father's name, my career, and my sons' futures—the future of all that I have worked so hard for would be destroyed. I can't let that happen, but this secret has become too much for an old man to bear and so I will write this.

"The night of the fire will live in my memory forever. It torments me even now. That night, Father had a terrible argument with Mr. Clarke. Clarke threatened my father. I was angry. With Father so close to winning the election, it made me furious that some worthless laborer would make false accusations against a man like my father. Father and I returned home that night, and I swore vengeance on Howard Clarke and his family.

"When my mother and father retired that night, I snuck out to seek my revenge. I waited until all was quiet and dark and then I tried to set fire to the barn. The timber was wet and I knocked into a feed can trying to find a suitable stick to light. The noise must have awakened Charlotte Clarke, for she was suddenly there, standing behind me in the snow, wearing only her night dress and boots. I ran—I didn't mean it to happen, but I threw the stick I had been attempting to light into the wood pile.

"Charlotte Clarke chased me into the hills. I ran toward Custard's Cavern—a cave Father and I had discovered the year before. The cave was my secret hide-out. She followed. Soon the house was engulfed in flames. The wonder of it—it lit the whole sky. Charlotte cried out and started for home, but I knew if she were to return, she would tell who had started the blaze. I chased her, quickly overcoming her. Being much larger than she, I caught her up and I pushed her into Custard's Cavern. Her neck broke when she hit the bottom. I rolled boulders over the entrance to hide her body. A blizzard came through that night, thankfully, and hid any evidence of our chase left behind in the snow.

"But for days I feared I would be found out. The townspeople searched the hills and woods, but she was never discovered. I fear for my family. If this secret were ever known, our family, our name so strong and powerful, would be ruined. We would be nothing. So, as years long past, and in the years to come, this secret is mine to bear. May God forgive me."

Logan finished and shut the journal gently as stunned silence stretched among the group. Logan stood thoughtfully and moved to the wide window. He stared out toward the yard, and Kadie watched his face closely. His jaw clenched.

"Poor Charlotte," she spoke.

"We can find her body now," Beth added.

Kadie's heart ached as she thought about the terrible death Charlotte had suffered. How tragic. She closed her eyes momentarily. Knowing the truth about Charlotte's murder was a relief, yet it left her feeling very sad for the young girl who lost her life so needlessly and for the family who met with such a tragic end. She smiled softly as a sudden peace filled her heart. They were together again.

Adelaide had rejoined her family. She had finally been reunited with Charlotte and Fred. Kadie knew the reunion would have been a joyous affair. Adelaide was home, and with the information Kenny Jukes had given them, they could find and bury Charlotte's body. She would rest in peace at last. Her body could be laid to rest next to her family, where she belonged.

Logan turned from the window. A smiled touched his lips as he spoke. "She deserves a proper burial. Once funeral arrangements have been made for Grandma, I'll see that Aunt Charlotte's remains are recovered."

"Wow!" Maysha cut in loudly. She turned to face Kadie with a scowl. "I will *never* let you step foot in another ghost town as long as I live." She shivered. "Ehhh—I think I'm going to go watch princess movies with Zaza. I need to dispel the heebie-jeebies."

Logan laughed quietly as Maysha pushed up from the couch and left the room with a flourish. Beth stood. "I think that's a good idea, Logan," Beth spoke quietly, then added, "I'll . . . uh . . . I think I'll go join Maysha and Zaza. A princess movie sounds great." She smiled.

Kadie watched in silence while Beth left her and Logan alone in the room. Her heart picked up pace as she turned slowly to face him. He watched her with a curious expression; his mouth quirked slightly.

"Well, what can I say?" He suddenly grinned. "Thank you for coming into our lives and bringing Aunt Charlotte's ghost with you." He laughed and moved closer toward her.

Kadie smiled and shrugged. "Well, it's definitely been a crazy couple of days."

Logan took another tentative step toward her. She held her

breath as his eyes bore intently into hers for several long moments, then he spoke, "It has." He paused. His smile faded. "And now you're leaving?"

Silence stretched between them, and Kadie swallowed hard before she nodded weakly. Sorrow tugged at her heart.

Logan's expression darkened as he went on. "I . . . ," His shoulders fell, and he shook his head. "Kadie, I think you know—I love you," he whispered.

Astonished, Kadie's lips parted. Her heart faltered, yet she felt as if it would fly through her chest. Her heartbeat quickened. His words left her breathless. She kept her eyes on his, and he smiled before he repeated, "I love you, Kadence Reynolds, and I can't stand the thought of you leaving—not today, not ever. I'm taking a huge risk, but I can't let you leave without at least trying to convince you to stay." Kadie stared, and the breath left her lungs in a rush when he added, "As my wife."

"Logan," she began, feeling stunned. She shook her head, feeling happily overwhelmed. The silence stretched between them, and his expression faltered just as Maysha's voice suddenly called from the hallway.

"Would you just say *yes* already?"

Kadie jumped and spun toward the door. "Maysha!"

Her sister's head popped around the door frame. "Don't get your knickers in a twist. I just came down to get some food! Now just say *yes* and be done with it! You've been gaga for the man since you laid eyes on him."

Kadie blushed furiously, and her cheeks burned hot. "Maysha—would you—*go!*"

Logan chuckled, and Maysha looked unrepentant. She tossed her hands in the air before she disappeared. Kadie inhaled. She rolled her eyes and groaned. Logan's hands touched her shoulder and he continued to chuckle as he turned her to face him.

"I'm sorry," she moaned. She didn't dare meet his eyes. Logan's mouth quirked in amusement, and she continued, "But she's right. I have been head-over-heels for you. I love you too, Logan. I love you—both of you. You and Zaza mean everything to me. The thought of leaving, it was tearing me apart. I couldn't bear the thought."

Logan pulled her in for a quick, hard kiss, and she smiled against his lips.

"I love you, Kadence Reynolds—ghosts and all, will you marry me?" he murmured.

Kadie nodded. "Yes," she whispered then leaned out of his embrace. "Yes!" she called loudly. "Did you hear that, Maysha?"

Logan laughed, and Maysha's muffled voice called in return, *"Finally!"*

Kadie rolled her eyes and shook her head. "Are you sure you know what you're getting yourself into?"

Logan grinned and kissed the tip of Kadie's nose. "No." He answered. "But therein lies the excitement."

PROLOGUE

"She's finally at peace," Kadie whispered as she bent to place a small bouquet of wildflowers on the new grave. She stood and stared down at the freshly turned earth. She sighed. This was Charlotte's grave, and she felt good knowing that Charlotte's body was where it belonged, right next to her family, who had died so long ago. "She's finally home."

"We owe her a lot, don't we?" Logan murmured.

The wind sighed through the large cottonwood trees that grew in the small cemetery, and Kadie glanced toward the surrounding hills. The little cemetery sat in the narrow valley between the juniper- and cedar-covered hills, just outside of Eureka, Utah. It had taken only a day for the authorities to locate Charlotte's remains once Logan had given them the information. A few weeks later, Charlotte's remaining bones had been released, and she and Logan had wasted no time arranging a proper burial. Logan and Kadie, newly married, had flown from Washington. Logan had ordered a new headstone and a local Latter-day Saint bishop had assisted in giving Charlotte a short memorial service.

Kadie took a deep breath and reached for Logan's hand. "Thank you," she whispered. She turned to her new husband with a smile.

His fingers closed against hers. "She brought you to me. She saved our daughter's life. It's the least I could do, huh?" Logan grinned, and she raised a hand to her stomach, trying to still the familiar butterflies.

Even after several weeks of marriage, Logan still made her feel giddy. She sighed and glanced out across the cemetery toward the wide, dirt parking lot. Maysha and Zaza were chasing a butterfly. The two laughed loudly with one another.

"I think Maysha has missed Zaza. She'll never admit it," Kadie voiced with a laugh.

"I think she's missed you too. Maybe we can still convince her to transfer to Washington State," he added. "If I promise a shopping trip to Seattle once a week, I think it will work."

Kadie caught his eye knowingly. "Maybe Beth would like a roommate now that she has her own place. They would have so much fun."

Logan nodded. "Well," his eyes fell toward the headstone. "It's done. They're all together again. And a new chapter in the Clarke family has just begun." He laughed. "I never thought I'd believe in ghosts! I'm still not certain if I do."

"Pessimist!" Kadie laughed.

He grinned and then offered, "Well, I do believe in miracles." He kissed her. "And you are my miracle."

"I definitely believe in miracles." Kadie smiled as they walked back toward the parking lot.

A breeze brushed past, and Kadie heard a sigh on the wind. She glanced back toward Charlotte's grave. The trees and bushes swayed with the breeze, and she smiled. No ghostly apparitions appeared to startle her, and everything was as it should be. Charlotte was finally home.

BOOK Club Questions for
Tide Ever Rising

1. Overall, how did you experience this book? What emotions did you experience while reading?

2. What characters do you admire? What are their primary characteristics and what did they bring to the story?

3. Why did Kadie feel such a desire to return Charlotte's journal to her family? If you found a similar object, what lengths, if any, would you take to return the item to its' rightful owner?

4. What does Charlotte's recurring image signify to you?

5. Do you believe in an afterlife and a spirit's ability to communicate from the grave? How does Charlotte communicate with Kadie?

6. How did the different viewpoints enhance the story?

7. Senator Jukes keeps a very dark secret. Why did he keep silent for so long and what repercussions would such a secret cause for him and his family?

ABOUT the *Author*

Mandi Slack grew up in Orangeville, Utah, where her father worked as a coal miner for eighteen years. In 1987 the coal mines shut down for a time and her father joined the US Army. They were stationed in Hanau, Germany, and she had the opportunity to explore Europe. Mandi's family returned to Utah in 1992, and they settled in Orangeville, Utah, where she attended and completed high school. She then attended the College of Eastern Utah, where she studied Geology.

Eventually Mandi changed her major and moved on to Utah State University while she completed a degree in special education. She then married her best friend, Charles Slack. They have three children, two dogs, and a lizard (sometimes several lizards).Their family loves to spend time together, and one of their favorite things to do is rock hound and camp. Her house is littered with rocks and minerals. Mandi loves the outdoors, and she enjoys writing suspenseful novels and short stories. You can contact Mandi through email at slackmandi@yahoo.com.